JOHN T. McMAHON'S
DIARY OF
THE 136TH NEW YORK
1861-1864

edited by
John Michael Priest

 White Mane Publishing Company, Inc.

Copyright © 1993 by John Michael Priest

ALL RIGHTS RESERVED — no part of this book may be reproduced in any form without permission in writing from the publisher, except by a reviewer who wishes to quote brief passages in connection with a review.

This White Mane Publishing Company, Inc. publication
was printed by
Beidel Printing House, Inc.
63 West Burd Street
Shippensburg, PA 17257 USA

In respect for the scholarship contained herein, the acid-free paper used in this book meets the guidelines for permanence and durability of the Committee on Production Guidelines for Book Longevity of the Council on Library resources.

For a complete list of available publications
please write
White Mane Publishing Company, Inc.
P.O. Box 152
Shippensburg, PA 17257 USA

Library of Congress Cataloging-in-Publication Data

McMahon, John T.
    [Diary of the 136th New York, 1861-1864]
    John T. McMahon's diary of the 136th New York, 1861-1864 / edited by John Michael Priest.
        p.   cm.
    Includes index.
    ISBN 0-942597-46-X : $24.95
    1. McMahon, John T.--Diaries.   2. United States. Army. New York Infantry Regiment, 136th (1862-1865)   3. New York (State)--History--Civil War, 1861-1865--Personal narratives.   4. United States--History--Civil War, 1861-1865--Personal narratives.   5. Soldiers--New York (State)--Diaries.   I. Priest, John M., 1949-   .
II. Title.
E523.5 136th.M33   1993
973.7'447'092--dc20   92-37207
                                                                               CIP

PRINTED IN THE UNITED STATES OF AMERICA

Table of Contents

Introduction v

Chapter I: **1861** 1

Chapter II: **1862** 12

Chapter III: **1863** 42

Chapter IV: **1864** 88

Postscript 121

Casualties and Losses of the 136th New York

    Appendices: A 122

                    B 124

                    Ć 125

                    D 126

                    E 127

                    F 131

Index 136

List of Illustrations

Map 1: **Virginia 1862-1863** 28

Map 2: **Gettysburg** 52

Map 3: **Atlanta Campaign 1864** 89

Map 4: **The Route of the 136th New York
         from Atanta to Savannah** 109

Captain Alvin T. Cole (Company A) 97

Lieutenant Edward Sill (Company K) 97

Introduction

John T. McMahon's diary (1861—1864) is one of those rare, subtle gems with which the self-achiever and the quiet person can readily identify. With the idealistic eyes of an impressionable, and deeply religious seventeen year old, McMahon meticulously captured the mindset of the Methodist Episcopal Church of Western New York. By tracking down the books which he read and the church members whom he identified in his diary, I have discovered a teenager who was reading Eusebius' *Church History*; Watson's sermons; Page's educational theory, and the Lives of the Saints (in Latin). Unable to go to school because his father could not afford to send him, he delved into his father's library, and with his father's guidance at home, he became well versed in theology, philosophy, and ethics.

The second chapter in the diary (1862) explains why John McMahon enlisted in the army, despite his calling to preach and teach. (He failed to mention that he lied about his age to enlist.) He recorded the events of the unfolding war as he heard about them through the newspapers. His regiment did a great deal of marching and picket duty.

The last two chapters (1863 and 1864) trace the regiment's campaigns from Chancellorsville through Atlanta. He included his observations of the "Mud March," Gettysburg, Lookout Mountain, Chattanooga, and Peach Tree Creek. McMahon covered them all from the perspective of a very average regiment—the 136th New York — through the eyes of a young sergeant.

The footnotes which acompany McMahon's pithy comments shed a great deal of light upon a regiment about which very little is known. At Chancellorsville, where the XI Corps was severely beaten, the 136th New York and its brigade lost six men. Gettysburg cost the New Yorkers over 100 casualties, several of whom were in McMahon's company. At Peach Tree Creek a member of the regiment won the Medal of Honor for capturing a Confederate flag. McMahon said the man was killed. He was right. A bullet glanced off the captured flagstaff and imbedded itself in the soldier's forehead.

This diary gives the reader a feeling of what it was like to outmaneuver the Confederates in Georgia while the rest of the army earned more glory and accumulated more casualties. Learn how the average soldier bedded down in the snow yet stayed warm. Keep a careful record of how often the average enlisted man bathed, washed his clothes, and received pay. Feel what it was like to have a comrade die and to be worried about his soul.

John T. McMahon's diary is filled with the commonplace and with a tremendous amount of humanity. By carefully tracing the records of the people he mentioned and by documenting the regiment's casualties as they daily occurred, I have shown the reader life as the average Christian soldier experienced it and documented the history of a little known regiment which fought to preserve the Union.

My special thanks to the Staff of the Special Collections Department, Manuscript Department, William R. Perkins Library, Duke University, who made the journal available to me for publication.

John Michael Priest

Chapter One

1861

September 27th, 1861.

    The rain is pouring down very fast today. I read in the [New York] Tribune to day the account of the state Fair held at Watertown, N.Y. There was nothing related worthy of note. The taking of Lexington by the rebels has caused a good deal of sorrow in the north.[1]

    Yesterday was the day appointed by the President of America [Abraham Lincoln] for fasting and prayer. I went in to the M. E. [Methodist Episcopal Church] at Lima, where I now live and heard a good [sermon by] Rev. Wm. H. Goodwin, D.D. I am beginning to read the Latin Bible.[2]

    My brother [William H. McMahon] is at home now to get recruits for his regiment.[3]

[September] 29th Sunday, [1861].

    In the morning I attended church at half past ten and heard [a] sermon from Rev. J. [John] M. Reid, D.D.[4] From Matt. 27: 3rd and 5th verses: "Then Judas, which had betrayed him, when he saw that he was condemned, repented himself, and brought again the thirty pieces [of silver] to the chief priests and elders, Saying, I have sinned in that I have betrayed the innocent blood, And they said, What is that to us? see thou to that. And he cast down the pieces of silver in the temple, and departed, and [went and] hanged himself."

    The Dr. began by saying it was remarkable that Christ chose Judas for one of his disciples knowing as he did all things and it was strange that he [Judas] should have become his follower. But he thought, as did the others, that Christ's kingdom was to be earthly and that he [Judas] would get both riches and honor by it. But he went and sold his Lord [for] thirty pieces of silver, about $20. We may say with safety that he thought (knowing as he did Christ's power) he should escape from the chief priests and elders and in that way should yet be ruler of the earth. I cannot say anything more about the sermon.

In the afternoon, I went to the College Hall and heard a sermon from the principal Prof. [Lewis] Hurd.[5] It was one of his very best. By the way, the people do not call him a good preacher.

Monday [September] 30th, [1861].

Father [Isaiah McMahon] and I are cutting corn today. The weather is cool and cloudy.[6]

October 1, Tuesday, [1861].

We will finish our corn today. The weather is quite warm. There has been no frost yet this fall, which is very remarkable.

Friday [October] 4th, [1861].

We commenced digging potatoes. The weather is mild and [there is] no frost yet.

Last night was the prayer meeting but I did not go because I was tired. O Lord, help me to become a better person and forbid that I should fall out by the way.

Sunday [October] 6, [1861].

It rained very hard in the forenoon. I went to church in the morning in the village and listened to a sermon by Brother [Joseph H.] Knowles.[7] And in the afternoon at College Hall, heard a discourse by Dr. [John M.] Reid. I am sorry that I have not time to put it all [down] which I remember of them. O Lord, help me to profit by them. In the evening we had a good prayer meeting at the church.

Tuesday [October] 8, [1861].

Last night it commenced raining, and continued until morning. Tonight is class meeting and I hope I can go. By the way, it is the wettest time I have ever known for this time [of] year.

Sunday [October] 13th, [1861].

Went this morning to meeting at the M. E. Church. The Rev. Fricker preached from Isaiah 6 and from the first to the ninth verse. He commenced by saying that with a Friend Divine the greatest wish he [Isaiah] had was to see God. The vision was typical of the coming Christ. I cannot remember it enough to write it down. He said for a man to see God was impossible for Moses could not behold him. Moses only beheld his goodness and he had to hide in the cleft of a rock.

Monday [October] 21st, [1861].

Last night there was a heavy frost. The first we have had this fall. For the two years past it has came about the 9th or 15th of September.

Tuesday [October 22, 1861].

Did not go to class meeting. I am trying to be good but I am come way short some times. O Lord, help me.

Wednesday, [October] 23, [1861].

It commenced raining about seven this morning. And we could not work. But I thought to improve my time by reading [David Perkins] Page's *Theory* and pray twain school keeping.[8] But father called and I must go.

The teacher should have good habits. And first he should not come before the family in which he lives, without washing and combing his hair. I do not mean he must dress rich for their wages will not admit of this. But they can be neat with what they have. He ought always, before coming into the school room, brush, comb [his hair] and wash his face and hands, clean his nails, and so forth. He should be courteous to all the pupils, wherever he meets them. The responsibility of a teacher is very great. Hence he should be careful not to do or say anything that would hurt the child. He should try to improve both the mind and soul. We must show them the beauty in their studies and get them interested in finding wisdom.

Thursday [October] 24th, [1861].

This morning it snowed a little. The weather is quite cold. We sacked some corn this forenoon and are going to dig potatoes this afternoon.

Sunday [October] 27th, [1861].

Went to meeting this morning. Heard a sermon from Rev. Mr. [Joseph H.] Knowles: The text [was] Col. 3:17. "And whatsoever you do in word or deed, do all in the name of the Lord Jesus." There are two ideas which are wrong in respect to our religion. But if we take the middle ground we are safe. The first doctrine says that we may do or say whatsoever we choose. The other, that the religion of Christ is a yoke of bitterness. And this reminded me of a conversation I had with a young man about religion. He would make a profession of faith if he could still enjoy himself but he thought this was impossible and I could not get his mind clear on this point.

But to come back to the sermon, he said we had the ability to come up to this standard, saying we are living in the manner of Christ and that we as a church should come up to this standard. And we must have Christ to come up to this measure. I have commenced to read the Bible through but of course, this is the second time. Lord, help me do Your will & to understand.

The weather is somewhat cold today.

Sunday, November 3rd, [1861].

Went to church this morning. The Rev. C. Glease preached from Matt. tenth chapter and thirtieth verse. "But the very hairs of your head are all numbered." The subject was the providence of God. Anyone that admits there is a God must admit He has a province, for the great God that created all things would not leave them to take care of themselves. Some theologians say that God made all things and made laws by which they are ruled and then left them.[9] But if you look at an engine we may admire its workmanship and its laws but this will not move with[out] some help. So it is in nature. The steam must be applied by him that made the laws or by some one that knows these laws. So it is in nature and no one but God knows these laws. And we may say that God rules the universe.

Monday, [November] 4th, [1861].

It has been cold and cloudy today. The news from the war is not very important. Our army is advancing slowly. They are within two miles of Fairfax Court House.

There has been a battle fought at Ball's Bluff in which we were badly whipped and Col. [Edward D.] Baker was killed.[10] He was Senator from Oregon and one of our best men. He might have been major general if he had wished it. But he could not be that and senator at the same time. He chose to remain senator rather than be made major general.

In the West, Gen. [John C.] Fremont is driving the rebels before him.[11] It was reported that General F. was removed but that is not so.

[McMahon erred on this point.] Gen. [Winfield] Scott has resigned on account of poor health and Gen. [George B.] McClellan takes his place.[12]

A naval expedition has just sailed to attack some part of the southern coast. There are eighty ships with thirty-four thousand men on board. We have not heard from the fleet yet.[13]

I have thought some of going to war but my father and mother [Margaret M. McMahon] would not consent to let me go.[14] They thought one son was enough from their family and beside all this, they wanted my help for they are in debt badly and have a good deal of work to do. I do not think it my duty at present to go to war. And I think until I see more clearly I shall not go.

Tuesday [November] 5th [1861].

We raked and drew in one third of our buckwheat today. I went to class meeting tonight, and the Lord blessed me. I am trying to live a holy and blameless life. Brother [Joseph H.] Knowles asked us to pray for his brother [Captain Daniel C. Knowles, Co. D, 48th NY] that is now at the war, as he's captain of a company and sailed with the expedition that has just gone out, that his life be preserved.[15] The thought came into my mind whether it was best to pray, that the lives of our friends should be spared.

We have been told that whatsoever we asked of God in the name of Christ believing, we should receive. If they die now, they may go to heaven but if they live they may go to hell. And there has been cases of the lives of persons being spared by praying earnestly when it was not for the best, and I remember of hearing a story of a woman having a son very sick, and she prayed that his life might be spared. She would not give him up but keeped praying and that until her son recovered but he was an idiot until the time of his death.

I might mention the case of a woman that had a boy very sick. She prayed that he might get well and would not think of such a thing as losing her boy. She prayed and prayed until he got well but within six weeks her husband died and with these facts before us I think we should say the will of the Lord be done in earth as it is in heaven. Amen. Amen.

Wensday [sic] [November] 6th [1861].

The weather is unfavorable for farming. It was rainy and foggy during the day. I went to the Lyceum debate this evening. It did not amount to much. One of the students of the college told me of a circumstance that happened in the hall this morning. A large gray dog came up on the steps before prayers and the boys got him into the hall before Prof.

L. came up and take his seat. Prof. W. [William Wells] came in and saw the dog.[16] He called him to come out. The dog came to the door and Prof. Wells went to kick the dog down stairs, but the dog caught him by the leg and all most pulled him on his face. At prayer time he came on the stage and made friends with Prof. Wells. After prayers were over one of the boys went on the stage to speak, the dog followed him up and when speaking, he walked around him and looked up in his face as knowing as he could. About this time Dr. [John M.] Reid came in and saw the dog. He looked very sober and seemed to think it was a sober matter. He got the dog to come to the door but could not get him to go out. The Dr. stood behind the door but it was no use. All this time Prof. L. and Prof. Wells were laughing together with the boys. The Dr. gave up the idea of getting him out and waited [until] the services were over.

Monday November 11th, [1861].

Yesterday was quarterly meeting. The love feast was good, but I have been to better ones. The P. E. [Presiding Elder] preached from Deut[eronomy] 32:31. "For their rock is not as our Rock, even our enemies themselves being judges." It was a good sermon but I was very sleepy, and cannot remember it very well.

In the afternoon [I] attended meeting at College Hall. Prof. L. preached from the text, "What think ye of Christ?" [Matt., 23:42] Prof. [Joseph H.] Knowles preached from first Peter 5:7. "Casting all our [your] care upon him; for he careth for you." He said there were two kinds of care. The one we should keep. The other [to] cast upon the Lord. We should have care for ourselves and care for the souls of those around us but we ought not to order our house about these things.

It rained some to day hard.

Wensday [sic] Nov. 13th, [1861].

There is considerable news from the seat of war. [In] Kentucky our forces, in a late battle, killed over one hundred and tooked a thousand prisoners.

We heard news from the expedition that they have taken two or three forts on the southern coast.[17] This will make the rebels feel bad.

December 1st Sunday, [1861].

Went to church in the morning and heard a good sermon from our pastor J. H. Knowles. First Deut. 32:9, and Lam. 3:24.[18]

It has been snowing nearly all day and the weather is quite cool.

Thursday Dec. 5th, [1861].

Commenced going to school to day at G. W. Sem. [Genesee Wesleyan Seminary].[19] I study Algebra, Geometry and Latin. I recite at eight, nine, and eleven.

[Friday] Dec. 27th, [1861].

The wind blows very hard, and [there is] a good deal of ice on the ground.

About ten days ago we had as fine [a] weather as I ever knew for the time of year.

Last Sunday Prof. Case preached at College Hall. His [text] was, "... men ought always to pray." [Luke, 18:1] He told what prayer was about and [about] the assurator of prayer.

I got up this morning at half past one and studied. We have very long lessons to learn.

FOOTNOTES — 1861

1. The Federal forces in Lexington, Missouri surrendered on September 20, 1861, following a three day siege, to Confederate forces under the command of General Sterling Price, C.S.A. *Battles and Leaders*, contains a unique account of the action by Colonel James A. Mulligan, who commanded the besieged Federal troops.
    Robert Underwood Johnson and Clarence C. Buel, (eds.), *Battles and Leaders of the Civil War*, Vol. I, (Secaucus: Castle), 307-313.

2. W. H. Goodwin was 45 years old and a Methodist clergyman.
    Entry for W. H. Goodwin, Livingston County, Lima, NY, Census of Population, (NA Microfilm, roll 778), Records of the Census, NA, Western New York.

    In 1800, Jonah Davis from Delaware founded the Methodist Episcopal Church in Lima in his home, which was three miles south of Lima Village.
    James H. Smith, *1687 History of Livingston County New York*, (Syracuse, NY: D. Mason & Co., 1881), 477.

3. William McMahon was 21 years old and a student.
    Entry for William C. McMahon, Livingston County, Lima, NY, Census of Population, (NA Microfilm, roll 778), Records of the Census, NA, Western New York.

    William H. McMahon, age 22, enlisted at Lima, New York on May 7, 1861 to serve two years; mustered in as Private, Company G, 27th New York Infantry on May 21, 1861; mustered in as 2nd Lieutenant, Company K, on September 11, 1862; mustered out with his company May 31, 1863 at Elmira, New York; Commissioned 2nd Lieutenant October 10, 1862 with rank from September 11, 1862 vice George S. Gaskill, promoted. Promoted to Captain, on October 26, 1866 for gallant and meritorious service in the late war. On December 30, 1868 he received the brevet rank of Major for gallant and meritorious service at Appomattox Court House, Virginia.
    Frederick Phisterer, (comp.), *New York in the War of the Rebellion 1861-1865*, 3rd Ed., Vols. I and III, (Albany: J. B. Lyon Co., State Printers, 1912), 346, and 2048-2049.

4. John Reid, age 40, was the President of Genesee College, Lima, New York.
    Entry for John M. Reid, Livingston County, Lima, NY, Census of Population, (NA Microfilm, roll 778), Records of the Census, NA, Western New York.

5. Lewis Hurd, age 38, served as the Principal of Genesee College.
    Entry for Lewis Hurd, Livingston County, Lima, NY, Census of Population, (NA Microfilm, roll 778), Records of the Census, NA, Western New York.

    The Methodists founded Genesee College in 1849 and erected College Hall the same year.
    (Smith, 1881, 474)

6. Irish born Isaiah McMahon, age 51, appeared in the 1860 census as a clergyman. He claimed $1800 in real estate and $800 in his personal estate.
    Entry for Isaiah McMahon, Livingston County, Lima, NY, Census of Population, (NA Microfilm, roll 778), Records of the Census, NA, Western New York.

7. Joseph H. Knowles, age 29, taught school at Genesee College.
    Entry for H. Knowles, Livingston County, Lima, NY, Census of Population, (NA Mircofilm, roll 778), Records of the Census, NA, Western New York.

Knowles was the pastor of the Methodist Episcopal Church from 1860-1862. (Smith, 1881, 479)

8. David Perkins Page — Born in Epping, NH, July 4, 1810; died January 1, 1848, of pneumonia. The son of a well to do father, who did not allow him to receive a formal education until he was sixteen years old, Page spent only several months in Hampton Academy in New Hampshire before he started teaching school. In 1829, he started his own school. By 1831 he was the assistant principal of Newburyport High School, where he chaired the English Department. Page taught himself Latin, and some Greek. He excelled in chemistry and mathematics, and possessed a thorough knowledge of history and literature.

    He married Susan Maria Lunt on December 16, 1832. From 1844 through 1847 he campaigned to implement the normal school system which Horace Mann and the State of Massachusetts had pioneered. Overexertion produced a short lived cold which quickly developed into pneumonia, from which he died within three days.

    In 1847, he published his only book: *The Theory and Practice of Teaching, or the Motives and Methods of Good School-Keeping.*

    Dumas Malone, (ed.), *Dictionary of American Biography*, Vol. VII, "Mills-Platner," (New York: Charles Scribner's Sons, 1934), 136-137.

9. John McMahon described Deism quite accurately. A belief structure popular during the 17th and the 18th Centuries among the erudite, including Benjamin Franklin, Thomas Jefferson, and George Washington, it recognized the existence of God and not much more. Deists did not believe in miracles, Divine intervention or formal religion. Jefferson, who wrote his own version of the *New Testament*, omitted all the miracles of Christ because he did not believe they happened. Deists believed in "reason," and the goodness of man, which runs contrary to the general Fundamentalist interpretation of Scripture.

10. On October 21, 1861, a badly mishandled Federal brigade (4 regiments and 3 artillery pieces) was soundly driven into the Potomac River at Ball's Bluff, Virginia by a Confederate brigade (4 regiments and 3 companies of cavalry) of about equal size. Colonel Edward D. Baker, who as of that date had not accepted the rank of Major-General, commanded the Federal troops and died during the action. The Federals lost 49 killed, 158 wounded, and 714 captured or missing. The Confederates lost 33 killed, 115 wounded, and 1 missing.
    (Johnson and Buell, II, 123-124)

    Edward Dickinson Baker (Born, London, England, February 24, 1811.) A self taught lawyer, veteran of the Black Hawk War and the Mexican War, and a personal friend of Abraham Lincoln, Senator Baker, in 1861, raised the "California Regiment" (71st Pennsylvania) from New York and Pennsylvania. He declined a brigadier generalship to become the regiment's colonel. When offered the rank of major general on September 21, 1861, he did not respond immediately. (To accept the rank he had to resign his Senatorial seat.) One month later to the day, he was killed at Ball's Bluff, Virginia, with the rank of colonel.

    Ezra J. Warner, *Generals in Blue* (Baton Rouge: Louisiana State University Press, 1981), 16.

11. The newspapers prematurely boasted of Fremont's success in Missouri. By November 1, 1861 John C. Fremont had herded Sterling Price's Confederate forces to Wilson's Creek, nine miles from Springfield, Missouri. Following two engagements at Fredericktown and Springfield, respectively, Fremont discovered that Price would not retreat any further. Rather than pitch,

immediately, into a battle, Fremont and Price met to negotiate the terms of the conflict. They decided to fight a conventional war among their own people.

Their agreement provided for the exchange of prisoners, despite the Federal government's orders not to do so, the suppression of guerilla warfare, which would leave the fighting to the organized, conventional armies, and the cessation of all civilian arrests for voicing their public opinions, which fell under the domain of the state courts.

On November 2, just before he prepared to give battle at Wilson's Creek, John C. Fremont was relieved of command by General David Hunter. The order, dated October 24, 1861, had been given by President Abraham Lincoln.

The order was not to be enforced if Fremont had fought a decisive battle or was prepared to fight one. Fremont said Lincoln's directive to that effect was disregarded. Hunter, pursuant to Lincoln's orders, withdrew the Federal force and discarded Fremont's agreement with Price. Lincoln wanted military victory and not maneuvering.

(Johnson and Buel, I, 278-288)

John Charles Fremont (born, Savannah, Georgia, January 21, 1813). Famous western explorer, army engineer, and U.S. Senator, Fremont received an appointment to a major generalship on May 14, 1861, in the U.S. Army. He failed in the Valley Campaign of 1862 and resigned because he refused to serve under John Pope, whom he strongly disliked. In 1864, rather than run against Lincoln as a Radical Republican, he withdrew from the Presidential race as part of a deal to get rid of cabinet member Montgomery Blair. He returned to California virtually bankrupt and was forced to depend upon his wife's writing career for most of his income.

Between 1878 and 1887 he served as the territorial governor of Arizona. In 1890, he was restored to major general in the army. He died in New York City on July 13, 1890.

(Warner, *Generals in Blue*, 1981, 160-161)

12. George Brinton McClellan (born, Philadelphia, PA, Dec. 3, 1826). McClellan served in the Mexican War as a brevet captain. Following the war, he served three years at West Point as an instructor. He also spent time at Fort Delaware, traveled in an expedition to the Red River, surveyed possible transcontinental railroad routes, and went overseas as an observer in the Crimean War. He resigned in 1855 to accept the job of chief engineer on the Illinois Central Railroad. By 1861, he was president of the Ohio & Mississippi Railroad.

On April 23, 1861 he became major general of Ohio Volunteers, from which he advanced to major general of U.S. Regulars, three weeks later. His victory at Rich Mountain, early in 1861, in the light of the disastrous loss at First Manassas, made it possible for him to become General-in-Chief of the Armies of the United States on November 1, 1861. He quickly and skillfully reorganized the demoralized army which had retreated to Washington, DC.

When his army failed to take Richmond during the Peninsula Campaign on 1862 and the Seven Days' Battles which followed, he lost the command of the army to Henry Halleck. John Pope took over the Army of the Potomac, which he had commanded briefly during the early days of the war.

After the Federal defeat at the Second Manassas, McClellan was given the command of the Army of the Potomac again. He retained that position until the end of the indecisive Maryland Campaign at which time (Nov. 7, 1862) he was ordered to give the Army to Ambrose Burnside. McClellan returned to Trenton, New Jersey to wait upon the country's call again. It never arrived.

In 1864, he unsuccessfully ran for the Presidency on the Democratic ticket. He resigned from the army on election day. After the war, he served as the Governor of New Jersey between 1878 and 1881. He died on October 29, 1885.

Winfield Scott (born near Petersburg, VA, June 13, 1786). Graduate of William and Mary College and hero of the War of 1812 where he served with the rank of brigadier general of Regulars, by 1861, he had served the United States as the commander-in-chief of the army from 1841 through 1861. A veteran of the Mexican War, the Mormon trouble in Utah, the nullification crisis in South Carolina, and the Cherokee resettlement to Oklahoma, he predicted a long, drawn out war. At age 75, he requested resignation from command on October 31, 1861. He died at West Point on May 29, 1866.
(Warner, *Generals in Blue*, 290-292, and 429-430)

13. Rear-Admiral Daniel Ammen, U.S.N., in "Du Pont and the Port Royal Expedition," left behind a very well written account of the article mentioned in the papers. The expedition had about 12,000 infantry on board. Its target, Port Royal, South Carolina, was part of the President's move to blockade the southern coastal ports.
(Johnson and Buel, I, 671-691)

14. Margaret McMahon, age 50, went on record as a housewife in the 1860 census.
Entry for Margaret M. McMahon, Livingston County, Lima, NY, Census of Population, (NA Microfilm, roll 778), Records of the Census, NA, Western New York.

15. Daniel C. Knowles, age 26, enrolled on August 13, 1861 in Brooklyn, New York to serve 3 years; mustered in as Captain of Company D, 48th New York Infantry on August 21, 1861; discharged on June 30, 1862; commissioned Captain on December 14, 1861 with rank of August 21, 1861, original.
(Phisterer, Vol. III, 1912, 2370)

16. William Wells, age 40, taught class at Genesee College.
Entry for William Wells, Livingston County, Lima, NY, Census of Population, (NA Microfilm, roll 778), Records of the Census, NA, Western New York.

Professor L. was not in census.

17. The two forts were Walker and Beauregard on Hilton Head and Phillips Island, respectively. They fell on November 7, 1861. The Federal navy lost 8 killed and 23 wounded, while the Confederates had 11 killed, 48 wounded, and 7 missing.
(Johnson and Buel, II, 671-691)

18. Deuteronomy 32:9.
"For the Lord's portion is his people; Jacob is the lot of his inheritance."
Lamentations 3:24
"The Lord is my portion, saith my soul; therefore will I hope in him."

19. The Seminary began in 1830. The first building went up in 1832. A co-educational institution it admitted 230 gentlemen and 111 ladies.
(Smith, 1881, 473-474)

Chapter Two

1862

Tuesday Feb. 4th [1862]

I have been sick with the diphtheria for about three weeks.[1] I was taken sick on Thursday the first [of January].

16th of Jan. My throat at first seemed smaller than [that of a] woman, and one side if it was a little lumpy and I could not swallow very well. I was also very cold. In two hours after I was taken I could not walk more than across my room. It was nearly two weeks before I could sit up much, and [if] I ate anything, it was very hard for me to drink water when sick, and even now it hurts me to. I have not been out of the house yet, though I hope to be able to [go out] soon. I do not expect to go to school any more this term.

My sister Laura was beginning to recover from sickness which was the diphtheria.[2] When I was taken she was sicker than I. But we were both sick enough.

I intend to commence studying very soon if I keep getting better, but I try to say the will of the Lord be done.

It was thought that Dr. [E. E. E.] Bragdon would not live last Saturday night but yesterday he was a little better.[3] He is in consumption.

Wednesday [February] 5th [1862]

My health is improving.

I have been reading the *Ecclesiastical History* of Eusevius [Eusebius] which gives one an account of the early Christians, their suffering, and deaths, and the way in which God sustained them in the hour of death, and made them choose death in any form rather than deny their God and savior.[4] When we read the history of those primitive Christians, that suffered every kind of persecution for the cause of Christ, ought not we to be thankful for the power the church enjoys at the present time?

I will now tell some of [the] ways in which they were tortured. Some were hung up by their feet, so that the hands would touch the ground, and then a fire would be kindled under them which would burn very slowly and in this way suffocate the persons. Again the feet of the person would be drawn just to two opposite limbs of a tree driven together by machinery and when the feet were thus fastened the limbs went back to their former position and, in that, wrenching the person asunder. Some were placed upon racks and had every limb stretched. Some had hot lead poured on their backs. But they could all say with [the] apostles, "We ought to obey God rather than men," and they could argue that they were counted worthy to suffer shame for his name. [Acts, 5:29]

I have been reading [Richard] Watson's sermon on Ezekiel's Vision of dry bones.[5] "Come from the four winds, O breath! and breathe upon these slain, that they may live." Ezekiel 37:9. He begins by saying, History informs us of the past, and our faculties of observing spread before us the scenes of present time, and this is all the information except what it has pleased God to reveal to us in his holy word.

It has been remarked by an ancient author that he who is acquainted with the past lives there. With equal truth it may be said he that is acquainted with the word of God lives there. We are not to suppose however that our view of the future after the most attentive study of the prophetical books, will be perfectly clear and satisfactory. It was a necessity with God that the prophecies were not made more plain, for as men we are to work out the plans of God, and at the same time be free moral agents, and in order to have this so prophecy must be somewhat dark. But as for this it is nonetheless true. This prophecy we think. First, it shows the condition of the heathen world. Secondly, it [is a] means to be used for their conversion. Thirdly, we may be sure that the use of these means will be successful.

Firstly, persons are represented as dead. It is the death of their souls & the number is very great. This valley is the whole world & the bones are unburied, showing that wickedness may be found in the day light and is not ashamed, for the prophet says the bones are very dry. By this we are to understand the hopelessness of their condition. Secondly, the prophet is told to prophesy upon the dry bones and say hear the word of the Lord, showing it is by preaching sinners are to be saved. Thirdly, we know that wherever the gospel is preached sinners are saved.

Thursday [February] 6th [1862]

My throat is not as well as it has been. It hurts me to swallow. Some other ways I am improving.

I have studied some today in my Latin. I find that since I have been sick a good deal of what I knew has left me. I have just finished reading Futeki's *Physical Geography*. It is a very fine work and worth the while of any young man to read it.

I also read one of Watson's sermons today. The subject was National Peace the Gift of God. "Lord, thou wilt ordain peace for us; for thou [also] hast wrought all our works in us." [Is., 26:12] We could not be assembled at any time more favorable than this. When peace has been given to us and war has ceased, we are called together to thank God for his peace.

In attempting to improve the solemnity of this day we shall consider it. What there is in the particular circumstances in our country to warrant us in considering the blessing as of special value and importance!! The ground of our acknowledgment of God on this occasion [is that] it is his work; he has "ordained peace for us," he has "wrought all our works for us." We are to examine what there is in the restoration of peace generally considered [to] excite our gratitude.

Friday [February] 7th [1862]

This morning my throat was quite sore and I was afraid that I should be sick again, but I feel as well as common now.

I studied my Latin some to day; it is up hill business for me. I have been reading about the ancient martyrs; there is one case especially worthy of notice. It is that of a young man named Apprianus, barely twenty years old and of a very wealthy family. He had the flesh scraped from his sides. His feet were burned in the fire. He was beaten with many stripes, and finally [was] cast into the sea. The author says it would seem to be impossible what he is going to relate but as all the people of Ceasarea were witnesses of it he will relate it. As soon as the youth was cast in to the sea there was heard a great sound. The earth was shaken, and at the time of this inhuman noise, the body rose out of the sea, and was cast before the gate of the city.

Sunday [February] 9th [1862]

It is a very unpleasant day. The wind blows very hard and drifts the snow into heaps, making it very unpleasant to be out doors. My father has gone to his preaching appointment today, which is about eight miles from here.

My throat is about as it has been. I think my health generally is improving. I am not able to attend church today. But I shall make the most of my time at home.

I have been reading some more about the Christian martyrs of old times. Among the numerous tortures they endured was to have the ankle of the left foot burned with a red hot iron and to have their right eye cut out and then burn the gaping hole with a red hot iron. But it may [ask] what was this done for; simply because they [were] Christians and would not acknowledge but one God. And [they] refused to sacrifice to the heathen gods. And yet amidst all of their sufferings they would "rejoice with unending great joy" knowing that great was their reward in heaven.

It is singular that the rulers and judges had no regard for age or sex. The old were tortured as badly as the young. The women suffered the same as the men.

One thing should be mentioned. That is [that] the bodies were not buried, but left for the dogs and the wild beasts and birds to eat. The soldiers watched the bodies so that their friends could not come and get the body and bury it. These rulers were not permitted to go [free]. The just vengeance of God overtook them all, and they died, suffering as much as those they had caused to be tortured. When the rulers began to think they must die they immediately stopped persecuting the Christians and wished all men to pray for them. We have but few crosses in these days to bear.

Monday [February] 10th [1862]

I have not studied much today. My throat is about the same. My health does not improve much.

Our folks have just captured Fort Henry in Tennessee.[6]

Thursday [February] 13th [1862]

My health is some better, but my eyes are very weak. I have been reading some in [Wooster] Beach's *Family Physician*.[7] I am going to try and do what he recommends for having good health, viz. live without eating meat, without tea or coffee, and without all kinds of rich food— "only leave the table feeling you could eat more." "Never eat between meals." "Keep clean and exercise a good deal."

Friday [February] 14th [1862]

I feel quite smart this morning, and my eyes are some stronger. I read in the "Northern" of this week, about some boys in the time of the Revolutionary War. In the autumn of 1776, in the village of Newark, Delaware, first as dark, a few boys between twelve and seventeen years of age were listening to James Wilson who was mounted on a barrel telling them of the sad battle of Brandeywine. James said, "If I could only get a gun, I would fight." One of the boys spoke out and asked if there were none in the place. James said he had been trying to find some but he could not find any, though he thought old Livingston had some, but [that] he would not let any come on his premises he could say for certain.

Frank Howard said, "Let us search his house." "That is a good plan," said James, "if there are any other boys that will go with me I will search old Livingston's place. All those that will go with me please come three steps forward." Everyone of the boys came out three steps. Old Livingston had a son named George and one of the boys said he could thrash him as quickly as that, and he snapped his finger to show how easy he would do it. On their way to old Livingston's house they met the old man's son. From him they learned that some men were at old Livingston's house and [they] were a going to come down the creek in a boat to burn Newark that night, and they would start in about an hour. They tied old Livingston's son hand and foot and put a handkerchief over his mouth so he could not haloo for help and then tied him to a tree. "Now," said James Wilson, "let us go to the stream and roll some big stones to the bank that overhangs the creek, and when the red coats come we will let them go down on them."

The boys in a short time had five large stones that would weigh half a ton each ready to roll off the bank. When the boat came down the stream Jim asked, "Who is there?" The men looked around [to] see where the noise came from and as the boat came to where the boys were, James shouted, "Cut loose in the name of liberty." Over went the rocks. They heard shrieks come up from beneath to tell them how well the plan had worked. Old Livingston's son in trying to get away was killed.

The old man's house was searched. Three barrels of powder was found, two field pieces and some guns. This was given to the Federal Forces. James Wilson and Frank Howard joined the army. Frank was killed in the battle of Eutaw Springs. James lost a leg at the siege of Yorktown and went home to his native village but mortifications ensued and he died with the [words] ever to be remembered on his lips— "Cut loose in the name of liberty."

Sunday [February 16, 1862]

My health is improving. I am going to meeting this after noon at College Hall. My eyes are very weak. I can hardly see to write or to read the coarsest print.

Tuesday [February] 18th [1862]

I am about the same—my eyes are quite weakened yet. It is hard for me to see to write.

We have received good news [of] our army. Fort Donelson in Tennessee has been taken and about fifteen thousand of the rebels made prisoners and four generals; they are [James Buchanan] Floyd, [Bushrod Rust] Johnson, [Gideon Johnson] Pillow, and [Simon Bolivar] Buckner.[8]

Roanoke Island in N.C. has also been captured and at least three thousand prisoners captured. When the news came [guns] were fired off and flags went up.

Sunday [February] 23rd [1862]

I am gaining in health very fast. I went to church this morning and heard a sermon from our pastor J. H. Knowles, A.M. [Master of Arts]. The text may be found in the eighth chapter of Romans and the 15th and 16th verses.[9] It was a good thing but my eyes are so poor that I can not see well enough to write something about it.

Our black horse died last night. His name was Jim. He was sick four days and suffered very much. He cost $90.00. It is quite a loss for us as we are now. But I can say the will of the Lord be done.

Sunday March 23rd [1862]

My health is quite good so I can study and read some. The Rev. Mr. Ives preached for Brother [Joseph H.] Knowles this morning from the text, "But if our gospel be lost, it is [hid] to them that are lost: In whom the god of this world hath blinded the minds of them which believe not, lest the light of the glorious gospel of Christ, who is the image of God should shine unto them. For we preach not ourselves, but Christ Jesus [the Lord]; and ourselves your servants for Jesus' sake." Which may be found in second Cor[inthians] IV and 3, 4, 5 verses.

He remarked that whatever god had made was glorious and the psalms described the glorious works of God, when he spake of the heavens as the handiwork of God. But his glory was seen most in the scheme of salvation which was made known to our first parents when God said the seed of the woman shall bruise the serpent's head. [Gen. 3:15][10] It was told Abraham also, and Jacob and David and all the holy prophets. And finally preached by Christ himself. It was the gospel of Jesus because he made it. It is the power of God unto the salvation of men.

I am going now to attend the funeral of Rev. E. E. E. Bragdon, D.D., Professor of Ancient Tongues in Genesee College. He died of consumption and is about fifty years old. Dr. Bragdon was born December 1812; he was the youngest of six boys. When a young man he learned the [darner's] trade and worked at it until he was of age. He then commenced studying. And in thirty nine received the degree of A.B. He paid his own way all of the time.

The cause of his death was this, when principal of a Seminary he was required to go out eight miles and preach a watch night sermon, but the Dr. was not satisfied with one and he delivered a second. This was too much for him. He came home weak. A severe cold and a cough allowed rum which he never received. He was a member of the B. R. Conference. He was the sound reassurer over his land too.

The Funeral sermon was delivered by the President of the College, Rev. John M. Reid, D.D.

[Wednesday] April 2nd [1862]

My sister, Sarah Jane McMahon, that was the second younger than I, was taken sick with the diphtheria on Saturday the 23rd of March and after being sick six days it went to her lungs and after suffering three more days she told us she could not live but asked us to meet her in heaven.[11] She said she was happy and Jesus called and she must go. She died after being sick nine days on the last day of March at nine o'clock in the year of our Lord 1862. She had her senses to the very last and said she was going to heaven. She spoke only about three minutes before she died; she died very easy and without crying.

She was 14 years 10 month and thirteen days [old]—weight was about 160 pounds.

Monday [April] 7th [1862]

Read this morning a sermon, "The death of Wilbur Fisk, D.D.," by P. Bangs, D.D.[12] It was on the church and the obligation and the character of a minister of the gospel. A minister should be well versed in human nature so as to understand the wants of the people he has the care of so to give to each a portion of the season. He should study in to the wants of his people and all of his learning should be made to serve the cause of Christ. Any learning that will not do is not worth having. There are fearful obligations resting upon the preacher for if he warn not the people then God requires their blood at his hand and he should not only warn them in the house of God but he ought to visit also in private by reasoning with sinners, by exhorting, by entreating and by prayer. He ought also to look after any that are growing lukewarm and [indifferent] to these things and exhort them to greater glory that they "may work out their own salvation with fear and trembling. For it is God which worketh in you both to will and to do of his good pleasure." [Ph. 2:12-13] He should be instant in season, out of season; reprove rebuke exhort with all longsuffering and doctrine always abounding in the work of the Lord. The character of a minister of the gospel.

The gospel means good news. That is it is good news from the Lord and he chooses men to proclaim this glorious gospel of Jesus Christ. The angels first proclaimed to the shepherds peace on earth good will to men. This gospel tells us our God is reconciled and his pardoning grace [is] here. Jesus is the author of this gospel. He came to this earth and was thought to be the son of Joseph the carpenter. He suffered and was tempted like as we are yet without sin. He died the death of the cross, was buried and rose [on] the third [day], ascended up in to glory and now [is] seated on the right hand of God the father. Christ died that we might live. That is the good news that the minister of Christ preaches to the world that Jesus Christ has passed on earth to forgiveness, forewarning one that preaches this gospel should be like the author of it—meek and lowly in spirit. His manner in the pulpit should be pleasing; his language refined; his reasoning sound; his manner earnest but if he has all this without the Holy Ghost, he preaches in vain.

Paul may plant. Apollos [may] water, but God gives the increase so that he that planteth is nothing neither he that watereth; but God giveth the increase. [I Cor. 3:6-7][13] The minister of Christ should understand this and, pray much that God would be with the word that he preaches.

He should know God from experience and the power of his appreciative hand that he can forgive sins and take away this heart of stone and give us a heart of flesh. He ought not to smile on the rich and not on the poor but should take each by the [hand] and encourage the weak in spiritual things to press on to perfection, comfort the sick the poor and the bereaved. He should be careful of the feelings of others; never offend a brother or accuse him until you know all and the case; it is better to pray with him before rebuking him.

Lastly, the [truth] of the gospel of Jesus Christ should be profoundly learned in the things of God and by this I mean he should be acquainted with nature, with the history of the religions in all ages, and with the different languages the Bible has been translated from especially the Hebrew, Greek, and Latin languages so as to explain any part of the Bible where the teaching is not plain.

He should be able to defend our Christianity against any foe and put the wicked to flight; he should pray without ceasing and in all things give thanks. I heard a minister of our church (a man that has been presiding elder several years) say in love first he regretted that he had not read the Bible more. This coming from such a man went to impress out minds with the necessity of reading the Bible. The minister should read his Bible and make it the sum of his counsel and, he will find this a powerful sword to wield.

When reason will fail of convincing a man then pray with him with faith. If this won't make him yield then nothing will, but the spirit of God can leave it in his hands. After praying and thinking over this matter, I have come to the conclusion that it is my duty to preach. I pray God that I may come up to this standard of a minister's life and be an honor to the cause of Christ. I hope I may soon be where I can study more than now.

There is a good revival going on here now. About forty have been converted and still this work goes on. May God bless the people.

Wednesday [April] 9th [1862]

This morning we found our one red heifer dead; she would have came in five or six weeks; she was two years old the 18th of March and was worth about eighteen dollars. Of a truth God's ways are not as our ways.

We have been treated this year very hard. My father has not received over $15.00 from his dairy this year and does not expect to get much more, and besides this, mother is not dairying.

Thursday [April] 15th [1862]

I have been working in the yard with father this morning; we been pulling up stumps and we set out amber; we have almost as good a yard as there is in this place. The only trouble is [that] it is not paid for, and there is but little chance of paying for it.

Monday May 16th [1862]

I have not been able to study for some time past or to write in this Journal on account of having so much work to do but now we are about through with our work and I expect to study some. I have read a little work on Christian perfection, and have been trying to come into this state. I think I can say I love the Lord more than these and my neighbor as myself. O Lord, create within me a clean heart and renew within me a right spirit. I wish to have this purity of heart without which no man can see the Lord.

Tuesday [May] 27th [1862]

Yesterday (26th) a young man came for ma to come and see Isabell, my sister, that is taken with the diphtheria.¹⁴ Mother has not got home yet so we do not know how she is. Father is going down this morning to see if she can ride home.

My brother is at home on furlough from his regiment. He is quite weak from the effect of his being sick. He was sick twelve weeks in the hospitals and the Dr. gave the order to lay him in the "dead room" to be washed and dressed for burial. But the nurse of the hospital would not do it but went to work and brought him to life.

I study every forenoon now and work afternoons.

My health is very good now.

Saturday [May] 31st [1862]

This morning [I] got up at five o'clock and milked the cow and now I am going to study.

Yesterday I read some *Natural Theology*. One would think that the man that studies nature would have to say there is a God. When we look at our own bodies we can see that there must have been some design when we were made. When we see how beautifully every part of our body is made and put together and how those parts that are the most tender are protected and then too if we lose any part of the body or any of our senses the others are much more perfect in order to help to restore the loss. But the hand of God may be seen in the arrangement of the several parts of the body. The eyes are just where we want them, [and] so with the hands, feet, mouth, and the same may be said of every part. Why not have the eyes on both sides of the head and the arms behind? The only way that we can tell why they are not so is because there is an all wise God.

Wednesday June 4th [1862]

This morning my brother returned to his regiment which is the 27 N.Y.V. He is third sergeant of Co. G.¹⁵ He came home to recruit his health which was very poor. He was sick in the hospitals twelve weeks. He goes back now in tolerable good health and feeling first rate.

I went to class meeting last night. There were a good number out, not withstanding the rain. Two sisters came over a mile in the rain and walked too. There are not many that will do this. I am studying now most of the time and I think that I am improving some. I study Latin every day and read to father. The grammar is easy for me to learn than to get a reading lesson.

Besides this, I read *Natural Theology*, which I like very much. I think the more I study the more I am convinced of there being a God and not only a God that made all things but a God that takes care of all thing and "up holds all things by the might of his power."

And I think that if the masses were educated more that Christianity would be far ahead of what it is now. I think this time will come, for schools are becoming more numerous every day. But if, in these schools, no attention is given to the training of the morals then but little good will come of them. We should be overrun with a lot of learned knaves.

But if our Seminaries and Colleges pay good attention to the students that are in them at this day and "bring them up in the way they should go" then our common schools will have Christian teachers and the coming generation will not be like this for then we shall have in a part what Isaiah prophesied of us. He says "For knowledge and wisdom shall be the stability of their times." [paraphrase of Is. 33:6]

Wednesday [June] 11th [1862]

Last night I was at class meeting. We had a good time and felt the spirit of God with us. A good many are trying to go on to perfection, and "to know the love of God which passeth understanding and to be filled with all the fullness of God." [paraphrase, Ep[hesians] 3:19][16] I am trying to live by faith on the son of God, and give all things into his hands.

I am studying now every day, and I think that I make good progress. Two weeks ago I could only read about half a page: now I can read over a page of Latin every day.

Thursday [June] 12th [1862]

I have been talking too much to my parents about sending me to school and I think I have not been as good as I should but by the help of God I intend to be better. I do not grow in grace as I wish to. For a time I seem to run well and then something happens to cross my path and I take offence & that I might overcome this evil spirit and lead a new life by faith on the son of God. When things are all right with me I am rejoicing but when temptation comes I am offended. This should not be. I want to be able to say thy will be done in all things with all my heart. O Lord, help me to live consistent with my profession that I may get to heaven.

[Sunday] June 29th [1862]

This day is the holy sabbath that God appointed for rest and the birds are singing in the trees, and all nature seems to be glad. I, for one, feel like taking rest for last week was a busy one.

It is near church time, and I am going. I am in hopes that I shall soon be able to preach the unsearchable riches of the gospel of Christ. I feel "woe is [unto] me if I preach not the gospel!" [I Cor. 9:16]

I want more learning, for I am very ignorant. My father does not feel able to send me to school now, but wants me to work for him.[17] The only thing I can do is to work, when he wants me to, and study whenever I can find time. It is very hard to come from the field tired and sit down to study a little while before going to work again. I very often fall asleep in my chair, when studying, but in all of this, thy will, O God be done and not mine.

[Tuesday] July 15th [1862]

The reason that I have not written more lately is that I have been very busy at my work.

This day is the first one on which I have studied for about six weeks, unless there was a rainy day, and that is the reason that I am studying today, because it has been raining.

There was a camp-meeting held on the second day of this month about two miles from here. I attended [it for] four days. It was a good meeting and I feel that I was blessed. My brother was in the last battle before Richmond, and came out all whole. Glory be unto God for this!

I am trying to live the life of the Christian that my last days may be like his. I think I can say that I am being perfected in Him. I love God with all my heart and my neighbor as myself. Praise God for this. Amen.

[Thursday] August 7th [1862]

The government has called for 300,000 men to volunteer and has given to the fifteenth of this month to enlist. If they are not ready by that time, they will be drafted.

Besides this 300,000 men, there are to be 300,000 more men drafted for nine months. Those that are drafted haven't the bounty. Now the question is, had I better go as a volunteer for three years and get the bounty of two hundred dollars, and the honor of going as a volunteer? (I should say that the drafts have but eleven dollars a month and the volunteers $16.00 a month.) Or go as a draft? (for it is quite likely I would be drafted for nine months without the bounty, and have but $11.00 a month, and have the disgrace of being drafted.)

If I should come home alive, and live to be old, I want to be able to say that I fought willingly for my country and not have my name branded as a coward.

As I have said before that I felt it my duty to preach, so I say now, and I have been studying as much as I could with this in view but the country calls for help, and I think now after praying over this subject day after day, and reasoning with myself, that it is my duty to go. I say it with a full heart, with the tears in my eyes, and in the sight of God.

I have thought that I might be killed or wounded, or taken prisoner, or die in the Hospitals, but none of this can alter my mind.

If the country is not saved then all is lost. There will be no need of a preacher, for the people would not hear. I believe if it is best that I should preach, then God will bring me, but God can so rule that every thing shall be to his glory. I pray God that His will overrule and guide me at all times, and finally bring me safe into the haven of eternal life for Christ's sake. Amen.

This is a part of what is in my heart. I have said what I thought to be the truth, and I will say "God's will be done."

Monday August 11th [1862]

I have enlisted to day in Captain [Alanson B.] Cornell's company at Lima, and expect to go into camp in a few days.[18] The company is made up of all classes of society, good bad, and indifferent. There are some good young men in it, and a good many bad ones. I hope to always cast my influence on the side of truth and religion and to live Godly in this present evil world There are some professors of religion in the company. Henry Weller, Mr. [George] Torrey, John Walldy, [and] Mr. [Fernando W.] Agard.[19] These are all that I know of, but I think some more will join.

Seth Buell is the Second Lieut.[20] I do not know whether the first [lieutenant] has been appointed yet. The noncommissioned officers have not been appointed from the ranks of the men. I think that I am as well as likely [to] be in as one of the Sergeants as any of the boys, but I may have a higher opinion of myself than others do, and while crying out "O that I was a ruler in the land." I do not care to be caught like Absalom in the branches of a tree, and die a miserable death while trying to get in a place for which I am not suited. I had rather be a private, and honored by the men than an officer and be hated by the men.

Saturday [August] 16th [1862]

This morning the Lima Company, Capt. Cornell's, in which I enlisted start for camp at Portage. We started from Lima at 6 A.M., and went to Honeoye Falls and from there by cars to an office where we changed cars for Portage, and then walked from the depot to the Barracks ¾ of a mile where we arrived at 11 A.M.

I am writing notes with the boys setting around me. I go [on] trying to live my religion.

Sunday [August] 17th [1862]

This does not seem like Sunday because the men train around. We are to be examined this morning by the Surgeon [Benjamin T. Kneeland] and if passed by him as sound, we will be mustered into the N.Y. Vols.[21]

Our rations in the morning consist of potatoes, bread, meat and coffee. About noon we have all but the coffee. Some times there are beans for dinner.

Last night I sleeped in the Barracks that are about all down. We had a little hay to put in the cracks. I had nothing to put over me except my shawl; it was a very cold night for that time of year, and I suffered from the cold. In the night some of the boys got up and run around the barracks to keep warm. Some of the men were in their shirt sleeves having left their coats at home.

It is now morning and the boys are putting up boards at the end of the barracks to keep out [the] cold. This afternoon we had a sermon at which all were present.[22] The army is no place for a decent man to be, but I have to submit for I think it my duty.

Monday [August] 18th [1862]

This morning I was put on guard for the first time. It is not hard. We are on two hours then off four.

This morning we had bread with maggots in it. The boys were so mad that they throwed it away. The great curse of a soldier's life is idleness.

Tuesday [August] 19th [1862]

This morning I was on guard for nearly four hours when I should have been on but two hours.

This afternoon I went into the Genesee River to bathe. It is the first time in over three years.[23] The banks of this river here at Portage are very high, and romantic. The bank opposite our camp is of solid rocks, and I should think two hundred feet high. You may throw a stone from the top of the bank and you cannot hear it when it strikes.

The bridge across this river for the R. R. is two hundred and thirty feet high, and about a quarter of a mile long. It is the greatest bridge about this part of the country.

The army is no place for a decent man. Such oaths and swearing

I never heard before, and such indecent language enough to make one blush for his honor.

Thursday [August] 21st [1862]

There has been some strange proceeding here. Our company and the company from Angelica has been consolidated. All those that were not of age, and did not have their parents' consent, were put out, and dismissed.[24]

Monday [August] 25th

I am home now on account of the division of our Company. Lieutenant [Seth] Buell was thrown out with us. He is expecting to take the rest of us, and get as many more as he can and join Captain [Henry B.] Jenks of Warsaw who has about 50 men. [Co. E, 136th New York][25] I might have been home to stay when I was thrown out, because I was not of age, and they could not hold me without my father's consent in writing, and this they did not have.

But I did not wish to come home in this way. When I come home, I wish to come with honor. Two young men have disgraced themselves already. Their names are M. D. Terwilliger and M. Decker. The former [was] a student in the Seminary. He enlisted, but was not sworn in, and when he was not put in as a Second Lieut. he ran home.

The night I came here one of the church wardens said, "Terwilliger ought to be hated out of town." I said, "If he goes back the boys would be for tarring and feathering him." He replied, "I should like to furnish the materials and help hold him." This was the general idea.

The other young caller here goes by the name of Eby. He tried to get in as First Lieut.

Sunday [August] 31st [1862]

I am now near the camp at Portage. This is the second Sunday I have been in camp as a soldier. The men that are making the barracks are working as on other days.

I went to the Presbyterian Church and heard a sermon on temperance. I can live in this. Obey.

Sunday [September] 7th [1862]

I am at home now. I came last Wednesday, and am going back tomorrow. My health is very good. I am going to church today . It may be the last time, for I may never come back again alive.[26]

Wednesday [September] 10th [1862]

Yesterday I came into camp about three o'clock, and walked thirteen miles. The Reg't. I expected to go in [130th New York], went away on Saturday. Our Reg't. [136th New York] will be ready in about two weeks. The barracks are now very comfortable. We have our woolen blankets and can sleep warm.

This morning I gave our Col. [James] Wood father's papers recommending him as a suitable person for the Chaplaincy of the Regt.[27] The Col. is a very fine [man], and is willing to speak to a private.[28] I am trying to live the life of a Christian.

Thursday [September] 11th [1862]

Our company has only a few men here. The rest are home for a few days, so we have to go on guard once in about two days.

This morning we had a good breakfast, and generally we have decent food. The other day I got some meat for the boys that stunk so [bad] I had to hold it at arm's length. I like this life better than at first.

Wednesday [September 17, 1862]

The Major [Davis C. Hartshorn] last week told four of us if we would work two days, he would give us five days furlough. I worked Friday, and Saturday. Then he said we [would] work Sunday. I did so, and he gave me seven days furlough, and besides he gives us pay for the work. (This last [time] he did not [pay] us.) I did not want to work on Sunday, but I had to.[29]

Thursday [October] 2nd [1862]

This morning we started for Washington with our whole Reg't..[30]

Saturday [October] 4th [1862]

At noon today we were in Washington. Went into the Soldiers' Rest for Supper, but the coffee was full of grease, and everything [was] so dirty the boys would not eat.

Marched to Arlington Heights, and got there at 9 P.M. We are without tents. Went to bed, or laid down without any supper.

VIRGINIA 1862-1863
Battles and Leaders of the Civil War, 1886

Sunday [October] 5th [1862]

Today we got some hard tack, and our tents [are] 9 by 9 feet, and ten [feet high].

Saturday [October] 11th [1862]

We have marching orders. The cooks are cooking two days' rations. We have been used rather hard.[31]

Monday October 13th [1862] Fairfax C. H. [Court House]

We started for this place yesterday morning with our knapsacks on, and two days rations in our haversacks. At night we camped in the woods about 4 miles from here, and ten [miles] from where we started.

In the middle of the night it rained very hard, and as I was on guard I had to stand and take it. When I came off of guard I laid down under a tree, and sleeped about three hours with the rain coming down on me. The ground was very wet. I had my overcoat on, but not my blanket on. It was the worst night I ever was out.

This morning we marched as soon as breakfast. Each one got his own meal, which was to cook some coffee, and eat our bread and meat. I am now resting in my tent. You see we marched on Sunday.

Sunday is not observed in the army. Each Sunday we have Inspection in the morning, and Dress Parade in the afternoon. The Battle of Bull Run was fought on Sunday and we were beaten, and so it has been at other times. I think that we must stop this before God will own us as his people. I hope to see the day when God's holy day will be keeped from the least unto the greatest.

Sunday [October] 26th [1862]

This morning it commenced to rain from the north east, with a cold wind—this continued all day, and night. We were in tents at night. I lay myself down to sleep. It was cold, and the rain beat against our tent which made me think of home, and a warm bed. I woke up towards morning, and found our tent almost down. I had to get up, and go out in the rain to peg it down.

Monday [October] 27th [1862]

This morning the rain stopped, but it was not long before it rained harder than ever, so that we could not cook our breakfast. At 10 A.M.

it stopped raining, and the sun came out. On the whole it was a hard time.

Tuesday [October] 28th [1862]

This morning I am on Pole Guard. My duty is to work. I have worked four hours. This is getting off easy.

I am trying to be a good boy, but there are no meetings for improvement. There has been but one meeting since we came into Va. [It was] on the 5th of October. I wish this thing were settled, and I could go home.

Friday [October] 31st [1862]

This morning the troops around here were reviewed by Secretary [of the Treasury, Salmon P.] Chase, and [his] daughter [Kate], who came here last night. There were two brigades on review. I expect that we will march in a day or two. The cooks are preparing food for two days. Some say we will go tomorrow.[32]

Sunday [November] 2nd [1862]

This morning our Reg't. took up the line of march for the enemy's country. We passed through Centreville, and camped four miles beyond it. I had two days rations in my haversack. It was hard tack, beef boiled, and tea, and coffee, and sugar.

At night I made tea, and with crackers made out a supper. Then [I] laid down on the ground to sleep.

At about 2 A.M. it rained some, but soon stopped.

Monday [November] 3rd [1862]

Marched as soon as we got our breakfast. We are to guard the wagon train. Thus we are in the rear of the army. We went through Hay Market, [which had] only about 6 or 8 houses, and passed over the Bull Run battle ground. I saw bullets and pieces of shell lying on the ground. We camped two miles beyond Gainsville—[which had] about 8 houses.

My health has been quite good and I feel thankful to God for it.[33]

Tuesday [November] 4th [1862]

We are in the same place, but do not know when we shall have to go on. We are within 2 miles of Thoroughfare Gap.[34]

Sunday [November] 9th [1862] At New Baltimore.

We came here Friday the 7th, and are going away this morning to Thoroughfare Gap.

We were at the Gap by noon, and are now settled again. Thus far we have always marched on Sunday, except once.[35]

Wednesday [November] 12th [1862]

We are to be mustered for pay this afternoon at two o'clock. I do not know how much I shall get but it is just three months since I enlisted. I have received one month's pay so that leaves two due me. I am to send ten dollars per month home so that will leave me three dollars per month.

My health is good and so are my spirits. I read the ninety-first Psalm this morning and felt much comforted.[36]

Monday [November] 17th [1862]

Last night we were ordered to load our guns and sleep with our arms, ready to fight at any moment. We are expected to be ready to march at any time.

I get along as well as common and feel pretty well. I wish that this war was over and I could go home.

Yesterday Uncle [Richard McMahon] was sent to the general hospital.[37] He has been sick some two weeks. I think he will be discharged and go home.

We are going to leave here at 4 P.M. We marched towards Fairfax C. H.[38]

Tuesday [November] 18th [1862]

Last night we marched but to Hay Market, two miles from the Gap. This morning we began to march at 8 A.M. and stopped at three o'clock within ten miles of Fairfax. After marching about ten miles today we passed over the battlefield of Bull Run. This is the second time for me to go over the ground.

Wednesday [November] 19th [1862]

Today marched at 8 A.M., and are now within about a mile and a half of Fairfax C. H.. Marched ten miles today.[39]

Sunday [November] 30th

We are at the same camp yet. The weather is not very cold; the ground freezes some at night but that was in the day time. We do not have much rain. Our Chaplain has preached but two sermons since his appointment.[40] We shall have no preaching today. I think he is of little use. I wish father had got the place but I do not want to have him down here to suffer as he would have to if he was Chaplain.

Uncle Richard died here in the Hospital and was buried in Fairfax. He was my father's brother and about forty-seven years old. He leaves a wife, and seven children and but little money.[41] He was one of six brothers and the first to die. The oldest is about sixty and the youngest thirty five.[42]

Tuesday [December] 9th [1862] In camp near Fairfax C. H., Va.

The weather is cold with some snow on the ground. We have the tents we left when we first commenced to march in this state. We are camped in a piece of pine woods and have been told we are to stay here for the winter. I have made our tent as comfortable as I could and in one corner I have made a fire place so it seems like living to be in it. The tent is nine feet square and there are three of us in it.

I am afraid our stay here will be short, for every little while I can see men going by on horse back with large envelopes in their hands. These are orders of some kind. Besides this all of the sick are being sent away from here. The orders have come for us to march in the morning with three days rations in our haversacks.

We shall have to leave our large tents and take the small ones on our backs. I do not like such usage. When you just get ready to live [you] have to pull stakes and move, but all I can do is to grin, and bear it. I cannot tell when or where we shall stop.[43]

Wednesday [December] 10th [1862]

This morning commenced to march at 8 A.M. The roads are frozen, so it is good walking but about noon the roads were muddy and bad. We have marched about 12 miles today and are in a piece of woods. We have made fires and cooked our suppers. There is some snow on the ground, so I shall have a cold bed. I scraped the snow off from the ground and lay down to sleep.[44]

Thursday [December] 11th [1862]

Today we have marched the same as yesterday. The roads are very muddy. I think we are on the road to Fredericksburg to reenforce Burnside's army.⁴⁵

Friday [December] 12th [1862]

Today we have come to a place called Dumfries.⁴⁶

Saturday [December] 13th [1862]

Today we went but five miles. So we had some time to rest.⁴⁷

Sunday [December] 14th [1862]

Today we went but about 8 miles.

Monday [December] 15th [1862]

Today we marched to within 2 miles of the city. [Fredericksburg, VA] (Distance 10 miles—J.J.M. 1862).⁴⁸

Tuesday [December] 16th [1862]

We are in camp now and do not know when we shall march again.⁴⁹

Sunday [December] 28th [1862]

Last night we left our camp after dark to get out as a reenforcement to our picket line and also to support a battery which has been planted on the banks of the river.⁵⁰

FOOTNOTES – 1862

1. Diphtheria is "an acute, infectious disease of the throat, usually accompanied by high fever and the formation of membranes that hinder breathing."
   The disease apparently causes suffocation because the membrane which develops in the throat is exceedingly hard and unyielding.
   Clarence L. Barnhart, (ed. in chief), *The World Book Encyclopedia Dictionary*, Vol. 1, "A-K," (Chicago: Field Enterprises Educational Corporation, 1964), 561.

2. S. L. [Laura] McMahon was 10 in 1860.
   Entry for S. L. McMahon, Livingston County, Lima, NY, Census of Population, (NA Microfilm, roll 778), Records of the Census, NA, Western New York.

3. E. E. E. Bragdon, age 47, taught at Genesee College.
   Entry for E. E. E. Bragdon, Livingston County, Lima, NY, Census of Population, (NA Microfilm, roll 778), Records of the Census, NA, Western New York.

4. Eusebius of Caesarea (c.263-339?) was the Palestinian born bishop of Palestine (314?-339). He signed the Nicene Creed. His 10 volume *Ecclesiastical History* is an invaluable source of early Church history. He preserved an irreplaceable collection of original manuscript material about the early Church. His *De martyribus Palaestinae*, (*The Martyrs of Palestine*), contains a complete list of the Christian martyrs in that Roman province.
   William Bridgwater and Elizabeth J. Sherwood, (eds.), *The Columbia Encyclopedia in One Volume*, (New York: Columbia University Press, 1950), 640.

   S. A. Cooke, et. al., *The Cambridge Ancient History*, Vol. XII, "The Imperial Crisis and Recovery, A.D. 193-324, (Cambridge: University Press, 1965), 712-713.

5. Richard Watson (1781-1833). The seventh of eighteen children he grew to what was then considered the gigantic height of 6'2". He preached his first sermon on February 23, 1796, one day after his fifteenth birthday and became a circuit rider as a Methodist preacher in 1801. Shortly thereafter he left the ministry to pursue a secular career in business and failed. He married the daughter of a Methodist preacher who belonged to the "new connexion" but a few years later he returned to Wesleyan Methodism.
   By 1812, he was working for an editor in Liverpool, at which time, as a reinstated Wesleyan minister, he became a leading supporter of Methodist missions. He also spoke out against slavery and drafted anti-slavery resolutions for the missionary committee (1825) which were adopted in 1830.
   His published works include: *Theological Institutes* (1823-1829); *Conversations for the Young* (1830); *Life of the Rev. John Wesley* (1831); *Biblical and Theological Dictionary* (1831); *An Exposition of St. Matthew and St. Mark, and of detached parts of scripture* (1833, posthumously published). Thomas Jackson edited *Watson's Work* (1834-1837 in 12 volumes).
   Sir Leslie Stephen and Sir Sidney Lee, (ed.), *The Dictionary of National Biography*, Vol. XX, "Ubaldini-Whewell," (London: Oxford University Press, 1964-1965), 938-940.

6. Fort Henry was fought on February 6, 1862. In the two hour fight against Federal gunboats in the Tennessee River, the Confederates lost 5 killed, 11 wounded, 5 missing and 94 captured, including General Lloyd Tilghman, captured. Less than 2,600 Confederates escaped to Fort Donelson. The Federal navy counted 7 killed, 27 wounded and 5 missing. A chance hit in the steam

pipe of the "Essex" caused most of the Northern casualties.

For details read the two good articles which appear in the pages cited below.

(Johnson and Buel, II, 358-372)

7. Beach, Wooster (1794-Jan. 28, 1868)

He was born in Trumbull, Connecticut where he received little formal education. Late in his teens he was apprenticed to a German herbalist and physician from Hunterdon County, New Jersey, Dr. Jacob Tidd, with whom he stayed until Tidd died in 1825, whereupon Beach moved to New York to attend the College of Physicians and Surgeons.

On March 7, 1832, he was elected to the New York County Medical Society. At age 31, he began writing prolifically. A rebellious and defiant individual who was prone to self-promotion and exaggeration, he vehemently opposed blood letting and purging with mercurials. He preached in defense of herbal remedies to cure most illnesses and he steadfastly refused to use a stethoscope.

In 1833, he published the three volume set, *The American Practice of Medicine*. It was the first systematic compendium of medical practice in the United States to correlate disease borne changes with the disease processes. Beach also founded the "Eclectic Medical Journal" in 1836 and in 1855 he became the president of the National Eclectic Medical Society; both institutions were still around in 1927.

In 1828 Wooster Beach opened the United States Infirmary in New York City and founded the New York Medical Academy. In 1823 he married Eliza de Grove and fathered 2 sons. The younger boy drowned which led to the doctor's mental and physical breakdown. He died shortly thereafter.

The Family Physician, 4th ed., 1844, apparently, was the book which John McMahon read.

Johnson, Allen, (ed.), *Dictionary of American Biography*,Vol. I, "Abbe-Brazer," (New York: Charles Scribner's Sons, 1964), 85-86.

8. John Buchanan Floyd, brigadier general C.S.A., did not get captured at Fort Donelson. He turned the command over to Gideon Pillow and escaped with his own forces.

Bushrod Rust Johnson, brigadier general C.S.A., was captured at Fort Donelson but later escaped.

Gideon Johnson Pillow, brigadier general C.S.A., finding himself in charge of a garrison which he could not save, handed the command at Fort Donelson over to Simon Buckner, then made his escape.

Simon Bolivar Buckner, brigadier general C.S.A., the commander at Fort Donelson, was captured and later exchanged.

Ezra J. Warner, *Generals in Gray*, (Baton Rouge: Louisiana State University Press, 1959), 89-90, 156-158, 241, 38-39.

9. "For ye have not received the spirit of bondage again to fear; but ye have received the Spirit of adoption, whereby we cry, Abba, Father. The Spirit itself beareth witness with our spirit, that we are the children of God."

Romans, 8:15-16. (King James Bible).

10. Gen. 3:15 (King James Bible).

In rebuking Satan, God said, "And I will put enmity between thee and the woman, and between thy seed and her seed; it shall bruise thy head, and thou shalt bruise his heel."

11. Sarah McMahon, age 12 in 1860, was born in New York.
    Entry for Sarah J. McMahon, Livingston County, Lima, NY, Census of Population, (NA Microfilm, roll 778), Records of the Census, NA, Western New York.

12. Wilbur Fisk (Aug. 31, 1792-Feb. 22, 1839).
    Born in Brattleboro, Vermont, the frail Wilbur suffered from pulmonary hemorrhages. A farm boy, with little formal education, he learned by independent study and by attending school in Peacham. He entered the sophomore class at the University of Vermont in 1812. He entered Brown and graduated in 1815. Raised in a fervent Methodist family, Fisk initially inclined toward being a worldly individual by seeking to become a lawyer but because of his early religious convictions, he declined to do so. He joined the New England Convention in 1818 and in 1820 became a full member. In 1822 he was ordained an elder.
    In 1823, Fisk married Ruth Peck of Providence, Rhode Island and became the first college educated minister in the American Methodist movement. As such, he did much to reduce the prejudice against further education. Between 1825 and 1830, he served as the principal of Wesleyan Academy, Wilbraham (CT) and as president of Wesleyan University, Middletown (CT), respectively.
    Fisk's early efforts to support education led to the creation of the Methodist Board of Education. He believed in temperance and helped form temperance societies. Besides this he promoted missions and though he detested slavery he did not support the Abolitionists. In 1835, he was sent to Europe to study educational institutions abroad and to recoup his health. Shortly after his return, his childhood ailment claimed his life.
    His biography can be found in Joseph Holdich, *The Life of Wilbur Fisk*, 1856. He wrote only one book, *Travels in Europe*, 1838.
    Allen Johnson and Dumas Malone, (eds.), *Dictionary of American Biography*, Vol. III, "Cushman-Fraser," (New York: Charles Scribner's Sons, 1959), 415-416.

13. This entry is a paraphrase of the following:
    "I have planted, Apollos watered; but God gave the increase. So then neither is he that planteth any thing, neither he that watereth; but God giveth the increase."
    I Corinthians 3:6-7. (King James Bible)

14. Isabell McMahon, age 7, appears on the 1860 census as a member of Richard McMahon's household. Perhaps she was boarding with Richard, who was John's uncle, at the time of the census. It is all together possible that Richard's wife, M. V. McMahon, being only 24, had agreed to raise Isabell to relieve the burden on her much older sister-in-law.
    It was not unusual for older parents to "farm out" their younger children to kinfolk to ease the financial burden upon one's relatives. I doubt that John, in his diary, would have mistakenly referred to Isabell as his "sister" if she were not.
    Entry for Isabell McMahon, Livingston County, Lima, NY, Census of Population, (NA Microfilm, roll 778), Records of the Census, NA, Western New York.

15. William McMahon's records in the Adjutant General's Report show him to have become a sergeant, but did not record the date.

16. "And to know the love of Christ, which passeth knowledge, that ye might be filled with all the fullness of God."
    Ephesians, 3:19. (King James Bible)

17. The 1860 census recorded John T. McMahon, age 16, as a farmer. He was born May 5, 1844.
    Entry for John T. McMahon, Livingston County, Lima, NY, Census of Population, (NA Microfilm, roll 778), Records of the Census, NA, Western New York.

18. Alanson B. Cornell enrolled at Portage for 3 years service; mustered in as Captain of Company G, 130th Infantry [1st New York Dragoons], on August 20, 1862; discharged for disability on October 8, 1862; resigned, October 9, 1862; commissioned Captain on November 1, 1862, with the rank from August 20, 1862, original.
    Regimental History of the First New York Dragoons, (Washington, D.C.: Gibson Brothers, Printers, 1865), 26.

    (Frederick Phisterer, II, 1912, 1154)

    John T. McMahon, standing at 6 feet tall, had a dark complexion, black hair, and black eyes and as such made a healthy looking specimen for the military.
    TAGO, Volunteer Organizations of the Civil War, New York 136th Inf., Field and Staff, "Descriptive Rolls," NA, Washington, DC, 145-146.

19. Fernando [Ferdinand] Agard, age 18 enlisted on August 8, 1862 in Lima, New York; mustered in as private, Company G, August 18, 1862 to serve 3 years; wounded in action August 11, 1864 at Newtown, VA; absent at muster out; no further record. He resided in Lima, New York after the war.
    Annual Report of the Adjutant General of the State of New York For the Year 1895, III, (Albany: Wynkoop, Hallenbeck, Crawford and Co., State Printers, 1896), 3.

    (*Regimental History of the First New York Dragoons*, 1865, 22, 48)

    Of the men listed by McMahon, Henry Weller, and John Walldy do not appear upon the rolls. They probably failed the physical and were sent home.
    David Henry Weller was not mustered into the 130th New York. On January 1, 1864, he enlisted in Company M, 8th New York Heavy Artillery. He died in action at Cold Harbor, Virginia on June 3, 1864 and was interred upon the battlefield. His widow and daughter were residing in Lima in 1881.
    A Record of the Commissioned Officers, Non-Commissioned Officers and Privates of the Regiments Which Were Organized in the State of New York, IV, (n.d.), 54-74.

    (Smith, 1881, 482)

20. Seth Parker Buell, age 29, enrolled at Portage to serve 3 years; mustered in as the Second Lieutenant of Company E, 136th Infantry, on September 3, 1862; mustered in as Captain of Company A on March 10, 1863; discharged on July 9, 1863; commissioned Second Lieutenant on October 4, 1862 with the rank from September 3, 1862, original and as Captain March 12, 1863 with rank from December 9, 1862, vice Alvin Thayer Cole, resigned. Buell resigned because of failing health. In 1881, he lived in Pittsburgh, Pennsylvania.
    (Phisterer, IV, 1912, 3586)

    (Smith 1881, 485)

21. Benjamin T. Kneeland was mustered in as major and surgeon on July 29, 1862 and mustered out on June 30, 1865.
    (Phisterer, II, 1912, 1149)

22. There is no way of identifying the chaplain who preached the sermon. The 130th New York did not have a chaplain.

23. Many people still believed that regular bathing caused illness. Quite typically, individuals would wash their hands, faces, and feet but not much else.

24. The 130th New York, in reality, had recruited two to three hundred more men than were allowed under the law. The 136th New York also over recruited to the tune of almost four hundred excess recruits who did not join the new regiment either.
    Lockwood R. Doty, (ed.), *History of Livingston County, New York*, (Jackson, Mich.: W. J. Van Deusen, Publisher, n.d.), 472.

25. Henry B. Jenks, age 35, enrolled at Middleburg, NY, on September 3, 1862 to serve 3 years; mustered in as the Captain of Company E, 136th New York Infantry, on the same day; discharged on March 13, 1863; commissioned as Captain on October 4, 1862 with his rank from September 3, 1862, original.
    (Phisterer, IV, 1912, 3589)

26. Discharged: 1 Lt. Myron Bartlett (Co. D).

27. James Wood, Jr., age 42, was appointed colonel of the 136th New York on August 8, 1862 at Albany, NY, to serve 3 years. He was mustered in on September 18, 1862. He mustered out with the regiment on June 13, 1865 near Washington, DC. He was breveted Major-General of U.S. Volunteers from March 13, 1865. He was commissioned Colonel on September 17, 1862, with rank from August 15, 1862, original.
    His regiment did not have a chaplain. The regiment eventually commissioned and/or appointed Alvin Thayer Cole, and George P. Folsom as chaplains, respectively, but neither served with the regiment.
    (Phisterer, IV, 1912, 3592)

28. The Federal army discouraged fraternization between the officers and the enlisted men. Routinely, a man had to go through his sergeant to speak to the captain and through the captain to speak to anyone of higher rank. At the Battle of the Wilderness, Captain Adams, who was captured by the Confederates noted how easily a Confederate colonel mixed with his men. He wrote, "I was somewhat amused by the camaraderie between the colonel and his men, it seemed so different from the reserve and distance which in our army was always shown between soldiers and their officers."
    Z. Boylston Adams, Cpt., Co. F, 56th Mass., "In the Wilderness," *Civil War Papers, Read Before the Commandery of Massachusetts, Military Order of the Loyal Legion of the United States*, II, (Boston: 1900), 373.

29. The 136th New York took two days to muster into the Federal service. On September 25, 1862 Companies B through I brought the following numbers into the volunteer service of the United States Army: B-102; C-97; D-92; E-98; F-97; G-90; H-95; I-99; and the Staff-7. [Private John T. McMahon (Co. E) age 18, lied about his age. The records show him being one year older.]
    On the following day, Companies A and K joined the army: A-96 and K-88. The regiment, counting the eight men who were mustered in August, now totaled 969 officers and enlisted men.
    Deserted: September 25 — Privates Warren F. Peck (Co. E) and Charles Shunway (Co. F).
    September 28 — Charles McGary (Co. C).

September 29 — Corporal Homer Churchill and Private Charles Harmon (both Co. A), Privates Jephthah Baker, Watson Hoxie, and Thomas Stack (all Co. D).
September 30 — Patrick Wrin (Co. F).
By now the regiment mustered around 958 officers and men, having lost to various causes 12 men in 6 days.

30. Deserted: Privates James Barnhart and Homer Britton (both Co. C), Anthony Casey (Co. F), Henry Cleveland, Patrick Danforth, and Albert Mosher (all Co. H).
Discharged with a disability: Private Morgan H. Thomas (Co. B).

31. Discharged with a disability: Private George Papson (Co. H).

32. By now the regiment had lost another 8 men and was down to about 950 men on the rolls of whom only 898 officers and enlisted personally could report for duty.
TAGO, Muster Rolls, Returns, Regimental Papers, Volunteer Organizations of the Civil War, Box 3295, New York, 136th Inf., Return for October 1862.

33. Discharged: Assistant Surgeon Charles Warner.

34. Died of disease: Captain Amos Davis (Co. K) became the first and only officer in the regiment to die of disease during the war. He succumbed to a high fever.
On November 8, 1st Lieutenants John J. Galbraith (Co. F) and Orange Sackett, Jr. (Co. G) were placed in arrest. Galbraith neglected to obey an order and failed to report company roll call for November 8. Sackett abandoned his post and after surrendering his sword to the adjutant found himself confined to quarters for five days.
TAGO, Regimental Orders and Guard Report Book, Civil War Organizations of the Civil War, New York, 136th Inf., R and P Office, 37.

35. Died: November 11 — Daniel E. Sunderlin (Co. G).

36. Psalm 91 [King James Bible]
"He that dwelleth in the secret place of the most High shall abide under the shadow of the Almighty./ I will say of the Lord, He is my refuge and my fortress: my God; in him will I trust./ Surely he will deliver thee from the snare of the fowler, and from the noisome pestilence./ He shall cover thee with his feathers, and under his wings shalt thou trust: his truth shall be thy shield and buckler./ Thou shalt not be afraid for the terror by night; nor for the arrow that flieth by day;/ Nor for the pestilence that walketh in darkness; nor for the destruction that wasteth at noonday./ A thousand shall fall at thy right hand; but it shall not come nigh thee./ Only with thine eyes shalt thou behold and see the reward of the wicked./ Because thou hast made the Lord, which is my refuge, even the most High, thy habitation;/ There shall be no evil befall thee, neither shall any plague come nigh thy dwelling./ For he shall give his angels charge over thee, to keep thee in thy ways./ They shall bear thee up in their hands, lest thou dash thy foot against a stone./ Thou shalt tread upon the lion and adder: the young lion and the dragon shalt thou trample under feet./ Because he hath set his love upon me, therefore will I deliver him: I will set him on high, because he hath known my name./ He shall call upon me, and I will answer him: I will be with him in trouble; I will deliver him, and honour him./ With long life will I satisfy him, and shew him my salvation."

Discharged with disabilities:
   November 14 — Lynus Reed, Jr., and George Suton (both Co. I).
   November 15 — George McDonald (Co. I).
Deserted: November 17 — Myron Webster (Co. G).

37. Richard McMahon, age 44, was born in Ireland. His name appeared as "McMahen" on the muster sheet.
   Entry for Richard McMahon, Livingston County, Lima, NY, Census of Population, (NA Microfilm, roll 778), Records of the Census, NA, Western New York.

38. Died: Alvarado Eastman (Co. A).

39. Deserted: November 21 — Ezra Higgins (Co. D).
   Died: November 25 — James Kiehle (Co. I).
      November 26 — Richard McMahon (Co. E) from typhoid and Sergeant Houghton Murray (Co. G) from unknown causes.
      November 28 — Myron W. Stoddard (Co. C) from typhoid.
   Discharged with disabilities:
      November 27 — Charles N. Pease (Co. B) and James Culvor (Co. D).
      November 29 — Nathan Elmer (Co. C) and William Munsee (Co. I).

40. Whoever the chaplain was, he did not appear on the rolls. Perhaps he belonged to one of the regiments in the brigade.

41. Richard McMahon, a jeweler, left behind his second wife, M. V. McMahon, age 24, and a native New Yorker and seven children—one of whom was probably his brother's daughter and one who was living as a farm laborer with another family in Lima.
   James McMahon, age 19, farm laborer, born in Ireland.
   Rachel McMahon, age 16, born in Canada.
   Joel McMahon, age 15, born in Canada.
   Nancy McMahon, age 12, born in Canada.
   Firsa McMahon, age 11, born in Canada.
   Albert McMahon, age 8, born in New York.
   Isabell McMahon, age 7, born in New York.

   Entry for Richard McMahon, Livingston County, Lima, NY, Census of Population, (NA Microfilm, roll 778), Records of the Census, NA, Western New York.

   Richard McMahon, who enlisted in Company E, 136th New York on September 20, 1862, died of typhoid fever at Fairfax Court House, Virginia on November 26, 1862. He was buried there.
   (Smith 1881, 484)

42. The regiment started to thin out rather drastically during the month of December, particularly from physical disabilities incurred by "hard service."
   Discharged with a disability:
      December 1 — Quartermaster Charles T. Horton.
      December 3 — Elliott Burr (Co. K).
      December 6 — John G. Sanger (Co. C).
   Deserted: December 3 — Lewis Dayton (Co. C).
      December 8 — Anthony T. Gannon (Co. G).
   Died of disease: December 4 — Norman J. Smith (Co. C).

According to the Muster rolls for November, the regiment had 664 present for duty. An additional 8 officers were sick and 6 more were on detached duty. 33 enlisted men were also on separate duty. The adjutant reported 41 soldiers absent without leave and 185 sick — a total of 273 absentees for that month.

TAGO, Muster Rolls, Returns, Regimental Papers, Volunteer Organizations of the Civil War, Box 3295, New York, 136th Inf., Return for November 1862.

43. Discharged with disabilities: Charles Smith, (Co. B) and Thomas Carroll (Co. H).

44. Died from lung inflammation: George W. Whitford (Co. E).

45. Died: Lafayette McFarlin (Co. I).

46. Discharged with disabilities: Cpt. Alvin Cole and Pvt. Alanson Scott (both Co. A).

47. Discharged with a disability: Daniel H. Thurstin (Co. A).
Deserted: Carlos Atwood and John McMartin (both Co. G).

48. Discharged with a disability: Isaac Aten (Co. C).

49. Discharged for a disability:
    December 16 — John Murray (Co. E).
    Died: December 17 — James C. Van Sickle (Co. C) and Hiram G. Wakeman (Co. A).
    December 22 — Louis Davie (Co. A), John Chapman (Co. E), Garry Atwood (Co. H), Duane Alger (Co. I).
    December 23 — from fever — Daniel Garthwait (Co. K).
    December 27 — William Grills (Co. C).
    Discharged: December 19 —. 1 Lt. John Galbraith (Co. F).
    December 23 — 1 Lt. Marshall M. Layden (Co. A).
    Discharged with disabilities:
    December 19 — Murray Brown and George Hollowell (both Co. C), and Cpl. Jerome Munger (Co. K).
    December 23 — Augustus F. Stearns (Co. H).

50. Discharged: December 28 — Johnathan K. Wixon (Co. K).
    December 30 — QM John T. Wright.
    Discharged with a disability:
    December 29 — Alonzo Eddy (Co. C) and Nathan Adams (Co. H).
    December 30 — James R. Wright (Co. H).
    December 31 — Carroll Van Rensselaer (Co. G).
    Died: December 31 — Louis Hann (Co. B) from typhoid.

To date, the 136th New York had been reduced by 74 effectives within 66 days for an average of a little over 1 man per day. The future did not loom any better. Once the regiment became involved in very severe campaigning, the attrition rate would increase dramatically. Officially, 921 men remained on the regimental books. Of those, 2 officers were detached from the regiment. 1 was on "French leave" and 4 were sick. 254 enlisted men remained absent from the ranks: 25 detached; 7 on leave; 38 AWOL; 185 sick.

Chapter Three

1863

Thursday [January] 1st [1863]

Our Regt. is still doing picket duty on the Rappahannock River. (This place is called Banks' Ford—J.T.M., 1865). We are fixing up our tents as comfortable as we can so I hope we shall stay some time here. I never was used as much like a brute as I have been here in the army but if my staying will help to close the war I am willing to suffer some but I think there is little hope of peace for some time to come.[1]

Monday [January] 26th [1863]

We are still in our old camp on the river. Last week Friday night I went out to dig on some breastworks; it was dark and rainy. The rain came from the northeast. I was out about three hours in the rain.

The next morning we were to attack the rebels, but it rained so hard that we could not do anything. The mud was so deep the cannons stuck in the road and could no be brought up and the pontoons were stuck so that whole regts. were detailed to guard them for fear the rebels would get across the river and destroy them. The rebels put up a flag with this on it, "Burnside's stuck in the mud."[2]

Commentary:

By the end of January the regiment had lost another forty men, thirty of whom were discharged for poor health or other reasons. Five men died from disease or other causes and four deserted. Enrollment stood at 879 officers and men, 250 of whom were not present for duty. 2 officers reported sick; 1 was on leave and another was detailed away from his company. 25 enlisted men were also doing duty away from the regiment. 1 was on leave. 43 had gone "over the hill." Hospitals held another 171 sick men and the provost guard had two under arrest. 28% of the regiment's book strength was not serving with it.[3]

Thursday [February] 5th [1863]

This morning we were woke up at 4 A.M. and told to be ready to march at 6. I got my breakfast and packed up my things by 5 o'clock.

It is a cold morning, with the wind in the northeast. Before day light it commenced to snow.

Six o'clock but no orders to move yet, and the snow flies fast. At 8 o'clock the orders came for us to strike our tents, and fall in line for a march [to] nobody knows where but each one has enough to keep his hands and feet warm. My boots are just the things for this.

We were marched 5 miles back from the river to the headquarters of the brigade; here everybody was on the move and I soon found out that all of [Franz] Sigel's men were to march back to Stafford C. H.

We had three days rations of hard tack and pork given us. We had to stand here so long that I got very cold. The snow still comes down very fast.

After about two hours we were ordered to move forward. At four o'clock we were halted on a piece of flat ground where the snow was three or four inches deep. I think this was the toughest show for a night's lodging I ever had.

I pitched my tent and went after some brush for my bed then got some supper, which consisted of a cup of coffee, a little fresh beef and four hard tack. I eat this then put my rubber blanket down on the brush I had brought and my over coat over it and rolling myself in my woolen blanket, lay down to sleep.

I was soon in the "land of nod" and thought myself at home standing in the kitchen door with mother in the kitchen and father on the porch, just as I used to do when I was at home and just going out to work. I thought too that father had killed a chicken and a turkey but before I had time to eat anything I awoke to hear the rain beating against my tent, for the snow had turned into rain.

I got up, packed away my things and cooked my breakfast which was the same as my supper. We came about seven miles yesterday.[4]

Friday [February] 6th [1863]

This morning the rain stopped and the sky looks quite clear. The roads are very muddy, so it will be hard marching.

We fell into line at noon and marched through mud almost up to our knees. Several times I almost pulled my boots off in the mud. This sacred soil of Virginia sticks more than I ever knew mud to in my life.

At five o'clock we came to within a mile of Stafford C. H. when we were halted in some thick pines where we have been ever since.[5]

[Sunday, February 15, 1863]

It is now the 15th of the month. I have a very good tent. It is raised up from the ground four feet with logs and then the tent [is] on the top. There is a good fireplace in the end of the tent and the bed is in the other end made of small poles with brush put on them.

The Pay Master came last night to pay our Regt. He pays up to the first of November from the time we enlisted. Our Company was paid this evening at nine P.M. I got $21.65 which was one month's pay and 17 days. That was the number of days I was in the service in August. I got one month's pay in advance so that makes $34.65 I have got in all. $15.00 came in an allotment paper which I will send home very soon. The pay master said he would pay us again the middle of next month. I suppose it will be two months pay, which will give me $20.00 to send home. I hope it will come in time to pay on the house the first of April.

Monday [February] 16th [1863]

Today our Division was reviewed by Maj. Gens. [Joseph] Hooker & F. [Franz] Sigel.[6]

Wednesday [February] 18th [1863]

Yesterday it snowed very hard all day and has now turned into rain. I am in my tent by a good fire and have some beans, and pork boiling for dinner and some dried apples cooking that I bought the other day. We have all the wood we want to burn for cutting it.

Last night we had such a hot fire that we could not get within five feet of it.[7]

Commentary:

February 1863 claimed another 35 soldiers, 28 of whom received medical or related discharges. 7 died. No one deserted. The rolls carried 842 officers and men. 4 Officers were on leave and 2 reported sick. The number of enlisted men on detached service increased to 34. 1 man still remained on leave. The number of AWOLs dropped to 39. The sick list went down to 129 soldiers and the number in arrest decreased to 1 man.[8]

Sunday [March] 8th [1863]

Today I am on guard in front of the Brigade Hd Qrs. The weather is unpleasant. At twelve at night it rained very hard but I did not come on until two when the rain stopped. The weather is very unsettled. It storms about every other day.[9]

Monday [March] 9th [1863]

Today I washed my clothes and also myself. It is one of the warmest days we have had this spring.[10]

Thursday [March] 12th [1863]

Today we are all out on picket for three days. I have got three loaves of bread, six potatoes and onions, half a pie, some cheese and enough dried apples for two messes.[11]

Sunday [March] 15th [1863]

We came in from picket today just in time to escape the storm that came. We had a very pleasant time while on picket.[12]

Friday [March] 20th [1863]

Today the snow begins to fly very fast. I am on guard again but I have it easier as I am acting as corporal of the guard.[13]

Saturday [March] 21st [1863]

The snow has fallen about six inches and still comes. This is what some call the Sunny South but I think this month [is] as cold here as at home. The snow has turned into rain which will make the roads as bad as ever. If it was not for this storm, I suppose we would have moved from here very soon. The more it rains the longer we shall lay still. So every time it rains I am glad, for I hate to put on my harness for a march worse than Cuff hates to have his put on.

Gen. [Adolph Wilhelm August Friedrich, Baron] Von Steinwehr has issued an order that each Company shall have two men to cook for the company and anyone found cooking shall be severely punished.[14] This order will be worth but little as quick as we commence to march, for then every man cooks for himself.[15]

Sunday [March] 22nd [1863]

It has stopped raining, but the clouds are very heavy yet and the roads are very muddy—about knee deep.

All I have to do is sit in my tent by a good fire. I wish I had the letters to read this morning or some of the many books father has at home but I have not.[16]

Friday [April] 10th [1863]

Today the President reviewed our Corps (the 11th Corps). There were over 20,000 persons present. The President was on horseback, and had a boy about ten riding on a pony by his side.[17] Then came Maj. Gens. [Joseph] Hooker & [Oliver Otis] Howard, the former Commanding the Army of the Potomac.[18] The latter [is] our Corps Commander and then [came] the Division Gens. with their staffs, and then enough bodyguards to cover him over twenty times if attacked. In this state he [Abraham Lincoln] rode by us with his hat off. He looks as if he had all he could attend to. I think by the time his time is up he will be ten years older than when he took his seat.[19]

Sunday [April] 26th [1863]

The Pay Master came today and is paying the men off as fast as he can. Our Co. was paid at nine P.M. I got fifty-two dollars—$52.00. Twelve of which is in money. The rest is in an allotment. The last Co. will not be paid until near morning. The reason we get our pay tonight is that we have orders to march in the morning, with eight days rations, which is five days more than we ever carried before.

Our overcoats have been sent to Washington for the summer, so we do not have to tug them.

Monday [April] 27th [1863]

I got up at half past three, packed up my knapsack, and haversack, got my breakfast and at 6 A.M. [we] were all ready to start.

We were soon on the way towards the rebels. The weather is fine and the roads good. We came about 15 miles. Which is farther than we ever marched before in one day.

I have got for the eight days nine pounds of hard bread, one of sugar, one half of coffee, two of pork. I think this is enough but we are to get some fresh beef. The cattle are driven along so as to save carrying that meat.[20]

Tuesday [April] 28th [1863]

This morning we were woke up at two o'clock, and at 5 A.M. [we]

were on the road. We are going to Kelly's Ford on the Rappahannock 30 miles above Fredericksburg. The 2nd, 5th and 11th Corps are going to cross at this point. We got to the river at noon and after resting until 2 P.M. we fell into line to cross.

At dark we came to the river, but the pontoons were not ready until midnight. Then we marched across and camped for the night.

The weather is foggy and the nights are unpleasant but this is part of soldiering.

Wednesday [April] 29th [1863]

We did not start away until noon on account of so many troops having to cross. Our Regt. was the first to cross so you see we are thought something of.

We marched about 5 miles into the country and just as we were coming out of a piece of woods the enemy opened on us with one piece of artillery. The first shot made the boys prick up their ears and hurry on as fast as possible. One shell hit the fence by the side of the road. One went between the first company and the guard and one passed over our heads. They shot about ten times at us but did no harm. We went on about five miles and camped for the night.

Just as I was going to sleep, the order came to fall in lines and take arms for our picket line had been fired on. After being in line an hour we went to bed and sleeped.

Thursday [April] 30th [1863]

It is raining quite hard, but we are on the march again. Today we came within nine miles of the rear of the city. [Fredericksburg].[21]

Friday [May] 1st [1863]

Today the battle has commenced. The firing of cannon is but two miles [distant]—the musketry is but a mile away. At five P.M. we were drawn into line, on a plank road and ordered to cap our guns, and to lie down on our faces. After dark we were moved down the road a piece and told to go to bed. All this time firing was going on between our advance, and the enemy—but we were not called.

The weather is very fine.

Saturday [May] 2nd [1863]

This morning we were moved behind a rifle pit and are waiting for them. Maj. Gen. Hooker and staff passed us this morning; he looks as though he had gained a victory already. The Gen. has them hemmed in on all sides and unless there is a McDowell with us, we shall gain the day. This afternoon at 4 o'clock our brigade went up into the woods, where the rebels were, to help some regts that had taken a rebel regt., to bring back the men.[22]

Wednesday [May] 6th [1863]

Yesterday it began to rain very hard from the N.E., and keeped it up all night. I was detailed for picket at one P.M. to stay out until morning. This morning the troops are all leaving and crossing the river. The troops were all taken away before the pickets were and I was one of the last to go away. We went to the river on a double quick for fear the rebels would take us before we got to our regt. Today we came about 18 miles through the mud and rain and camped in the woods. We are going right straight for our old camp at Stafford C. H.[23]

Thursday [May] 7th [1863]

I am now in camp safe, and sound after march of 80 miles [since April 27]. We came [at] 7 this morning. I do not know how much we have made, nor have I time to discuss the subject but one thing is certain I lost all I had but what was on my back. This, however, I will get all back from the government.[24]

Friday [May] 8th [1863]

There is nothing going on today. The weather is still unpleasant with some rain.[25]

Saturday [May] 9th [1863]

This morning I washed my clothes and myself so I am clean again. We got new tents today in place of those we lost.[26]

Thursday [May] 28th [1863]

Things have been going on as common until yesterday, when we marched into some wood a quarter of a mile from our old camp. We had built up logs four feet high, and put our tents on them. Our beds are made of round poles. We have two beds, and two sleep in a bed. I worked yesterday so hard I came near being sick and then went on guard at night. The weather has been very warm some of the time.[27]

Thursday [June] 4th [1863]

This morning at half past two A.M. we were woke up and told to be ready at three to march. At half past four we were marching but we only went to the breastworks, less than a quarter of a mile. We stayed until five and then marched back to camp with the idea we were got out to see how quick we could [deploy] if attacked.[28]

Wednesday [June] 10th

Our Regt was paid two months pay today. (I got $26.00 -J.T.M 1865). There is some talk of moving but I can not tell how much it will amount to.

Friday [June] 12th [1863]

About ten A.M. we got orders to march at one P.M. We started at this time and take the road to Hartwood Church, which place we made at sun down. I went in search of water to cook my supper. It seemed as if every creek was dried up but after walking about an hour I came to water. We are very hard to be found and we have to depend on springs and creeks. I never sweat so in all my life. We came 12 miles.[29]

Saturday [June] 13th [1863]

This morning I was woke up by the bugles before four and at five we were on the road. We came about 15 miles and stopped for dinner. The dust is very plenty and we have to walk right in a cloud of it. Tonight we stopped at a small place called Weverville. This is called 23 miles from where we started this morning. This is the largest march we ever made in one day.[30]

Sunday [June] 14th [1863]

We began to march at nine and at three P.M., [and] stopped for two hours at Bristoe Station. Then we were on the road until one at night.

Today we came 20 miles. We would not have been so long on the road but the first three hours we went only about two miles, but after that we made good time.

Yesterday and today the boys fell out very fast. I saw some fall down as they were walking unable to go farther but I keeped up all of the time. It is hard work to kill me, for I am tough. We are going toward Maryland as fast as possible.

Monday [June] 15th [1863]

This morning we drew three days rations and then commenced to march. At nine we came to Centreville—a distance about five miles, where we are yet. I think we shall stay here tonight. We have come 63 miles in all in 2½ days which I think is well for such hot weather.

Tuesday [June] 16th [1863]

Last night I saw Mr. Beckly, Mrs. Wells' brother. He is in the 126th N.Y. Vols., Co. D. I had quite a long talk with him. They look a good deal cleaner than we do. His health is quite good but he had the measles last winter. I find but few have as good health as I do all the time. Soldiering agrees better with my health, than with my feeling.

Wednesday [June] 17th [1863]

Last night I was on guard at Brig. H. Qtr., and at three this morning was sent to my Regt. When I got there I found every one getting ready to march and at four A.M. was on the road to Leesburg.
About one P.M. it was so hot I came near wilting. I fell sick to my stomach but we soon came on to the road where the wind blew a fresh gale and I was all right again. We stopped for the night at Goose Creek on a large farm, where [there] were a flock of sheep. Our Co. got about five of them which is enough for us. I have had all I want to eat and have about 3½ pounds boiled to eat yet. The boys went out and killed them without leave or license.
We came 23 miles today.

Thursday [June] 18th [1863]

This morning I woke up just as it was getting light and found most of the boys ready to march and I got ready too. We fell in, and took arms and counted off but for some reason did not go and are here yet. I washed and dried my shirt. It was very hot in the forenoon but this afternoon it is raining. We are within 6 miles of Leesburg.

Friday [June] 19th [1863]

Today the weather is quite cool with some rain. We are in the same camp yet.

Saturday [June] 20th [1863]

It rained quite hard last night and raised the creek so that we had to come back across the creek to the Washington side for fear of the bridge being taken away and thus cut off our retreat. Our brigade was the only one on that side [of] the creek. It has rained some today.

Wednesday [June] 24th [1863]

This morning I went on guard and at eleven we packed up and started for Edwards' Ferry. We got there at five o'clock but as the distance was but two miles I did not mind going on guard in the morning.

Thursday [June] 25th [1863]

This morning we crossed the Potomac River into Maryland, just nine months from the time I was mustered into the U.S. Service. It was nine A.M. when we crossed. We went 30 miles today to a place called Jefferson. In coming here we came through Poolesville with our flags flying. The women cheered us and waved their handkerchiefs well. This is the first place for them to do so.

It began to rain at four P.M. and rained all night so the ground was very wet. This is the longest march we ever made in one day and my feet got quite sore.

Friday [June] 26th [1863]

We did not start until noon today and went about 7 miles to Middletown, where we camped for the night.

Saturday [June] 27th [1863]

This morning [I] felt very sick and unable to march but at ten o'clock we had to pack up and go to what is called South Mountain Pass, about 6 miles off. I never marched when it was harder work for me. We had dress parade tonight and I went out. I thought I should fall down; I was so sick.

Sunday [June] 28th [1863]

This morning I went down to the spring and washed me. When I got back I was all tired out. This afternoon at 4 we started again to march. I feel some better. We marched until 11 P.M. and stopped at Frederick City.

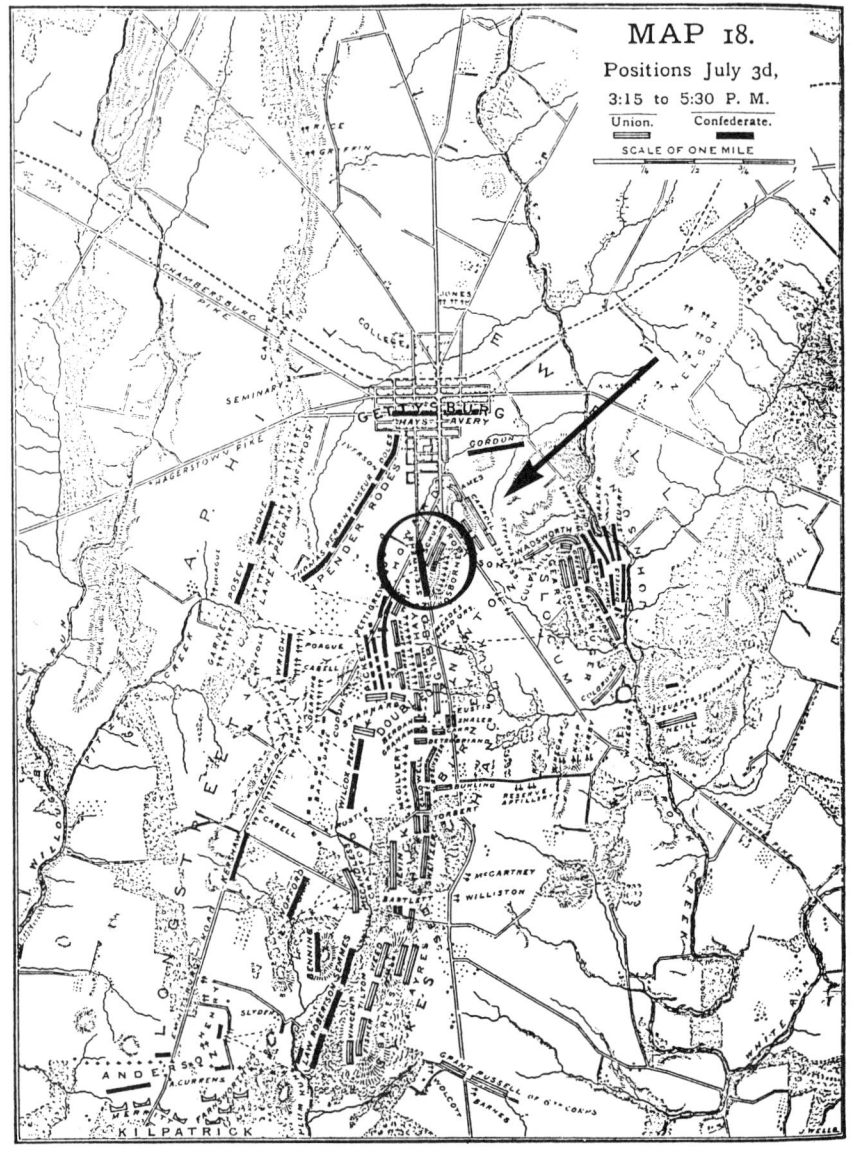

POSITION OF THE 136TH NEW YORK AT GETTYSBURG
Battles and Leaders of the Civil War, 1886

Monday [June] 29th [1863]

We were on the road at half past four this morning, without supper or breakfast. We had no time to cook. We stopped two hours for dinner and at 4 P.M. camped for the night. We have been on the road 24 hours and gone over a distance of 38 miles. This march has made me feel well again. My feet are very sore.

The country through here is the best I have ever seen. It will beat our land at home. There is a great deal of wheat growing here, more for the same amount of land than is raised at home.

We are now at Emmitsburg near St. Mary's College.[31]

Wednesday [July] 1st [1863]

This morning we started at 7½ A.M. and went into Pennsylvania to Gettysburg. I think it is about fifteen miles from where we started. When we came here we found that there was quite a battle going on. We went right up for support but today have not fought any. We have had six men wounded in our Regt. today. One will die I think. One belonged to our Company.[32]

Thursday [July] 2nd [1863]

Today we were sent out as skirmishers (our co.) for 2 hours. We had one man, a Corp. [John Fiero], very badly wounded and two [Patrick Duffy and one unrecorded] were wounded a little. I came out all right. The balls fell around me pretty fast. Just as soon as you put your head in sight they would fire at you.

At four and a half this afternoon the fight began along the whole line very fury. The rebels advanced on us and then such a firing of cannon and guns I never heard before. The fight continued until ten at night, when the rebels fell back to their old place. I think the rebels were whipped pretty well.[33]

Friday [July] 3rd [1863]

At two P.M. the fight began again. Today I was in it. For half an hour the rebels tried to drive in our lines but were drove back. We took three flags from them and one whole brigade of the rebels were taken prisoners. We had our Sergeant, [James Hanigan] and two privates killed [James Doren and Lelotas C. Wiggins]. One of the privates lived until the next day but the other two men were shot dead at once. I was hit by a ball that tore my pants and went down into my boot, without doing me any more harm. James Lavery of Lima was wounded but I think will get well.[34]

Saturday [July] 4th [1863]

This is a new way for me to spend the fourth. There is no fighting going on today of any consequence. We think the rebs have [had] enough.[35]

Sunday [July] 5th [1863]

Last night our Co. went out on the skirmish line. It rained some of the time very hard. In the night you could hear the wounded groan on the battle field; some have been there for 36 hours: some of the poor fellows cried out for some one to kill them; they were in such pain. The rebels are all gone this morning, and I have been over some of the battle field.

The rebels are four to our one on the field; the cause of this is that we had a cross fire of artillery, and musketry on them, where they tried to advance, and take out artillery.

This is the first battle field I ever went over and never want to see another. I pray God that this wicked rebellion will soon end. I suppose we shall follow them as fast as we can go. Our cavalry are now after them.

The 11th Corps has got a good name this time. Our boys all fought well this time. Lt. [Bishop Hamlin] True [Co. E] did well; he took a gun, and fought like a man.[36]

Tonight at five we started from Gettysburg and marched until 11 P.M., when we stopped for the night. We are on the road to Emmitsburg, Md. We had to march in one rank. The road was so cut up by the rain and troops coming to the battle. I was glad to leave for the stench was getting so very bad, enough to make one sick.[37]

Monday [July] 6th [1863]

Today we got to Emmitsburg where we stayed for the night.

Tuesday [July] 7th [1863]

Today we went 26 miles to a place called Little Rock. My feet are very sore. All I have for supper is a cup of coffee.[38]

Wednesday [July] 8th [1863]

This morning we were off at five and without my breakfast. We marched to Middletown where we got rations at noon. This is 24 hours without eating and marching hard too but I do not mind this if we only get old Lee, and his army. I filled myself with hard tack and beef if I ever did. We stopped at Turner's Gap near to Boonsboro for the night.[39]

Thursday [July] 9th [1863]

This morning I got a pair of shoes & two pair of stockings. I threw away my boots. They made my feet so sore. Now I can march all day & not get lame.[40]

Friday [July] 10th [1863]

At ten A.M. our Regt. was on the road again. We went about five miles towards Funkstown, where we stayed for the night. When we were coming here we could hear cannon firing very plain but by the time we got here the rebs had gone.[41]

Saturday [July] 11th [1863]

This is the first day for 3 or 4 weeks for us to stay in one place. Some times we have not moved more than a mile but today we have not been moved.[42]

Sunday [July] 12th [1863]

This morning we can hear artillery in the direction of Hagerstown but do not know what it is for. At noon we left our camp and went about 5 miles to within a mile of Hagerstown. At dark we commenced to build breastworks in front of our Regt. Each Co. made its own. We first made cribs of rails and then filled them with dirt.[43]

Monday [July] 13th [1863]

Our Co. went out on the skirmish line this morning but were keeped as a reserve. There has been some firing today but no one [was] hurt. We are all ready for a battle.[44]

Tuesday [July] 14th [1863]

This morning the rebels are crossing the Potomac. We can hear the sound of cannon. I think the enemy will have a hard time of it. We went 6 miles beyond Hagerstown and to within 4 [miles] of the river. Hagerstown might be called a city, I think; there are about 10,000 inhabitants in the town. It rained some this afternoon.

Wednesday [July] 15th [1863]

This morning we were woke up by three and by five were on the road to Hagerstown. We marched to within ½ miles of Middletown when we camped for the night at 8 P.M. Distance 21 miles.

The day was very warm and we had to go very slow. I feel well all of the time. My feet are well.[45]

Thursday [July] 16th [1863]

This morning we were again on the road at five [in the morning] and passed through Middletown and Jefferson, then turned on to the road leading to Harper's Ferry. We left this road and went about two miles to the left where we camped for the night.

It is now noon. We are about ten miles from the Ferry. As soon as I eat my dinner I went to the creek and washed my shirt, drawers & myself.

When we first came in here we had only about ²/₃ of our Regt.; the others had fallen out. You see by this we [are] pretty well tired out. I think we shall stay here and rest for a day, or two.

I got a letter from home today dated the 5th of July. I got some blueberries about half ripe and cooked them. They made very good sauce. I feel first rate.

Friday [July] 17th [1863]

It rained quite hard last night & some this morning. I think we shall stay here today.

Saturday [July] 18th [1863]

Today I saw some of the boys from the 130th N.Y.V. I was in that Regt. at first.

Mr. [George E.] Torry is acting as orderly in the Lima Co. [Co. G].[46] [Guilford] Wiley Wells is first Lt.[47] John, the boy that worked for [George Henry] Chappell, is well but I did not see him.[48] I saw Mr. Jones' stepson. He is well. I saw Charley Harding of Mt. Morris.[49] Mr. [Henry] Gale is 2nd Lt. in that Co. [Co. B].[50] He used to go to school with me. Mr. [Charles] House is in this Regt.[51]

Sunday [July] 19th [1863]

This morning at five we went across the Potomac at Berlin and went to within three miles of Leesburg. 16 miles we made today. We stopped at noon in a large field of blackberries. I picked a quart of them for dinner.

At night we had all we wanted to eat. I got my cap full and a quart besides. The fields are full of running blackberries. I never saw berries so thick in all my life. It was impossible to step without getting on them. The boys killed a sheep and I got a piece.

Monday [July] 20th [1863]

At 5½ A.M. we were on the road and went 10 miles and stopped for dinner. Here I got my two cups full of berries again. After resting 3 hours we went on 5 miles & camped. Here the boys killed both sheep & hogs. I got all the fresh pork I wanted for two meals. If the folks are secesh our officers do not say [a] thing against our getting all we can to eat. Right here they are not very good Union folks.

Sunday, when we passed through a small town called Waterford a little girl cried out, "Three cheers for the victorious army that is coming." The people through here are pretty loyal but on Monday they were altogether different.

When we were in Md. we went through a town a few hours after the rebels had and out of one house we saw a flag flying. Some of the boys asked the man what he did with the flag when the rebs went through. He said he'd had it in the straw bed. I think it is a wonder that any one will cheer us, or look at us, for the dirtiest man that ever walked the street of Lima is no comparison to us soldiers. We are dirty from head to foot and besides are black as Indians & ragged or as the boy "Dirty ragged, & saucy."

However the people seem to appreciate what we are doing for them and show it in waving their hats & flags but you go to buy a loaf of bread & they went from $0.25 to $0.50 & sometimes even more. I gave over $0.25 for three pints of milk and skimmed at that. All are not so. I had rather be in Va. where I can get things without buying them.

Tuesday [July] 21st [1863]

Today we are resting. I do not know what to call this place. We are on Goose Creek & about 4 miles from Aldie.

Wednesday [July] 22nd [1863]

Today things go on as common. I think we shall leave here soon.[52]

Thursday [July] 23rd [1863]

This morning we were off before five without any breakfast & went

7 miles & stopped for breakfast. After ¾ of an hour we went on 8 miles to White Plains & stayed two hours for dinner. From there [we] went to New Bottom. In 10 miles we got here at 6 P.M.

There are no houses here; our army burned them all last fall, except 3, or four and there is not a fence to be seen. We were within a mile of here last fall, before we went to Thoroughfare Gap.[53]

Friday [July] 24th [1863]

Today moved camp into the woods and expect to stay here sometime. Tonight I went on picket.[54]

Saturday [July] 25th [1863]

At midnight the bugles began to blow, and at three we were called in. At five we were on the road to Catlett Station, which place we reached at noon & went into camp. Distance 15 miles.[55]

Sunday [July] 26th [1863]

Everything is quiet today & we are allowed to rest, a thing we cannot enjoy every Sunday. I read two of Mr. [John] Wesley's Sermons today—one on faith & one on conscience. I liked them very much and got some new ideas. The way I came by them was this. Lieut. [Bishop] True [Co. E] found a volume out in the field & he took and gave the sermons away to those that wanted them. I got one or two. I should have taken the book but it was too heavy to carry.

Monday [July] 27th [1863]

Today I am on guard at Brig Hd. Qrs. We are about half way between Catlett Station & Warrenton Junction.[56]

Tuesday [July] 28th [1863]

Today I washed my clothes & wrote to Isabell [his sister].

Wednesday [July] 29th [1863]

Nothing new today—everything quiet.[57]

Thursday [July] 30th and Friday [July] 31st [1863]

[I] am some sick today. We moved our camp about 2 miles today.[58]

Saturday [August] 1st [1863]

This morning at 2 we got orders to march in 2 hours. I got up just in time to get my things ready. I do not feel any better. I did not eat any thing before starting. We were on the road at five [in the morning] to go to Brintsville—15 miles.

About 10 o'clock it began to be very hot. I felt worse as the heat increased. By 11 A.M. the men began to fall out. Some were sun struck. One man died in less than five minutes after he fell down. We rested in every piece of woods we could find. I began to think I should fall down. I was very dizzy. When the Reg't. stopped to rest I lay down and did not go on with it but rested ½ hour. I got to the Reg't. two hours after it had camped. I made some coffee and eat some and it made me feel better. This was 4 P.M.

I was called out on picket at 6 P.M. The Regt. had but 60 men when it first camped but by night the boys were about all in. I never knew such a hot day.[59]

Sunday [August] 2nd [1863]

Today feel better but very weak. I came in from picket at dark. I was told we were to stay all summer here.

Monday [August] 3rd [1863]

This morning we came back to Catlett Station but came on a nearer road. We got here at 10 A.M. Today was not so warm. Distance 10 miles. I feel well, but worn out with work.

Tuesday [August] 4th [1863]

We are in camp and expect to stay some time.

Wednesday [August] 5th [1863]

Today I fixed my tent by raising it 2 feet and making a bed up from the ground. I am about well today. We got soft bread for the first time since the 5th of June.

Thursday [August] 6th [1863]

[I] am on camp guard today.

Sunday [August] 9th [1863]

Today we had preaching. The man [preacher] was about 6 feet high and well built but nothing very extra on a sermon. His text was "Come unto me, all ye that are weary, and heavy laden, and I will give you rest." [Matt. 11:28, paraphrase.]

Monday [August] 10th [1863]

Today we get two months pay up to the first of July—$26.00.

Tuesday [August] 11th [1863]

Today has been very warm. The weather is more steady than in N.Y.S. As for heat, I never knew such hot weather at home. It would be impossible to carry on a campaign in this month.[60]

Friday [August] 14th [1863]

Last night an order was read to our Company as follows: "Corporal John T. McMahon is here by promoted to the rank of Sergeant to fill the place of James Hanigin who was killed in the battle of Gettysburg." The promotion is to date from July 3rd.

I did not expect this. I shall get $17.00 per month instead of $13.00.

Sunday [August] 16th [1863]

This morning I went to hear the chaplain of the 33rd Mass. Reg't. preach.[61] We did not take more than 15 minutes & closed by prayer. His subject was [about] the effect that Christianity has upon the government when it [the government] acknowledged [Christianity]. I have come to the conclusion that our Chaplains are a class of men that could not get employment at home and by underhanded work have got to be Chaplains. At any rate I never heard a good sermon from a Chaplain yet.

I had a good nap this afternoon and woke up with a letter from home. I think Mr. Hall has got a pretty wife but he would have had a better one if he had got Miss Bush who he used to pay his respects to, but he may think different.[62]

Monday [August] 17th [1863]

This morning at three our Reg't. sent out pickets. Our Co. sent 7 men and a Corp. [corporal]. This with the camp guard detail leaves the Companies so small that we do not drill. We present but 44 enlisted men, 5 Sergeants, 5 Corporals, 2 Buglers, 2 cooks, 2 Officers' waiters and out of these 1 Sergeant sick and one man and 1 Corporal sick, leaving 4 Sergeants, 4 Corporals, and 27 privates that are [fit] for duty, and to carry guns. There are a few wounded and sick in the Hospitals that may come back to the Co.—say about 10. It may be seen by this that we are in need of some conscripts to fill up our ranks.

I am troubled some in reading with my eyes as I was at home. I have to stop and look off of my book for a little while, when I can see as well as ever for perhaps ten minutes when I am almost blind again. It is impossible for me to read at night. This has come on within a week and as far as I know without a cause.[63]

[Tuesday, August] 18th [1863]

Last night at 6 P.M. we were on the move again after being in this camp 2 weeks. We were in the rear of the train so that we did not get over the road very fast. We camped at midnight at Bristoe Station—10 miles from where we started. It was a nice night and we got along well.[64]

Thursday [August 20, 1863]

There is quite a change here in the night from warm to cold. For sometime past we have had very warm nights but now they are cold, and [with] very heavy dews. We will soon need overcoats and woolen blankets.

Our Reg't. guards the railroads about 7 miles—from this Station to within 3 miles of Catlett Station. About 30 men guard at a time for three days.[65]

Sunday [August] 23rd [1863]

This morning at 6 A.M. [we] left our camp and marched to Greenwich—7 miles. We came to guard this place. (It belongs to an English man and there are about 8 or 10 houses besides his—J.T.M., 1865.)

Wednesday [August] 26th [1863]

Last night I was Serg't. of the Bristoe Patrol. I had ten men with me. We went half way to the Station when we meet the Patrol from Bristoe and stayed ½ hour when we came back. This road is one that the guerilla watch to capture all that come in their way.[66]

Saturday [August] 29th [1863]

Today I am on picket. The duty is not very hard. I have 8 men & two Corps. After we were out 4 hours we were called in to get ready to march but we were ordered out again and we shall not go I think. It rained some this morning but it has cleared away and is pleasant.[67]

Sunday [August] 30th [1863]

This morning at 5 were relieved by the 75th Penn. Vol. which reg't. has come to take our place. We are ordered to Manassas Junction to guard on the railroad.

We started at 7 A.M. and were at the Junction at 12 A.M. We went to Greenwich [on] one Sunday and left on the next Sunday. This was a good place to stay, for the folks are some Union.

One man [a civilian] told me that our Regt. was the first camp he ever was in of ours. [He] said he was afraid at first but, "Your Col. and men used me so well I forgot any fright and now I like to talk with them." The people think we came to eat them up and leave neither root or branch. From here to Greenwich is 11 miles.

Monday [August] 31st [1863]

Today we were mustered for pay (two months). We are only ½ mile from the camp of the 130th N.Y.V. They are in the cavalry now [1st New York Dragoons].[68]

I am glad now I did not go in that Reg't., for I do not like the cavalry service.[69]

Tuesday [September] 1st [1863]

[I] had new potatoes today. For the first time, my ration was four.

I went over to the 130th N.Y.V. I saw Mr. [Henry] Gale. He is 1st Lieut. in the Mt. Morris Co. [Co. B]. Mr. [George E.] Torrey is Orderly Sergeant in the Lima Co. [Co. G]. I saw [Sgt.] Charles Harding [Co. B] and [Pvt. Charles] House [Co. B]. They are both well. Mr. Rier the [2 words unclear] is not very well.[70]

Friday [September] 4th [1863]

Today went on picket for three days. We have an old log house to stay in. It has a fire place and we can cook in it and live home fashion—only we have to sleep on the floor instead of in bed.[71]

Saturday [September] 5th [1863]

I am in the old log house yet. We had a Major and [a] Sergeant of cavalry stay with us last night. I had a good fire all last night made of rails. The nights are quite cold.[72]

Monday [September] 7th [1863]

This morning we have been relieved from picket and went into camp. Tonight our Co. had to go out as reserve pickets. This will make four nights for me to be out.[73]

Tuesday [September] 8th [1863]

Today I got my haversack full of apples to make sauce. I went about 2 miles after them.

Friday [September] 11th [1863]

Last night I got a letter from Tsin and answered it today. Our duties are quite hard here. But I have it easier as the Sergts. are not called on as often as the Corps. or privates are. This is a thing that ought to be attended to for the poor privates will have to wear their lives out doing duty while the Corps. does less, and the Sergts. still less. The duty ought to be made equal or nearly so.[74]

Wednesday [September] 16th [1863]

All is quiet on the Potomac. I have nothing important which to write.[75]

Saturday [September] 19th [1863]

Today, I am on picket duty until 12, when I went to bed and the other Sergt. was on duty. Every thing was quiet and we were not disturbed through the night.

Tuesday [September] 22nd [1863]

Today, [I] came in off picket. We were paid today. I got $28.80.[76]

Wednesday [September] 23rd [1863]

Today I am resting. Our camp is at Manassas Junction. I sleeped a little this afternoon. It was quite frosty last night. This morning the sun has come out warm.

Thursday [September] 24th [1863]

This afternoon we went to Bristoe Station, 4 miles. When we got there we were told that in the morning we were to take the cars for Alexandria but at 11 P.M., [we] were called up and marched back to camp.

Friday [September] 25th [1863]

We are waiting for the cars. At 8 A.M. [we] went on board for some place. No one knows where.

Went through Alexandria, Washington and before we came to Baltimore, turned off that road and took the one going through Berlin, Harper's Ferry, Martinsburg, Farmington and Cumberland to within 4 miles of Wheeling, Va.[77]

It is Sunday [September] 27th [1863]

We are now in Ohio at Bridgeport. We have been on the cars for fifty-six hours and are now off getting our dinner.

Sunday afternoon [September] 27th, [we] got on the cars on the Ohio side at 2 P.M. We were cheered by all as we passed. The men cheer for [John] Bough the union candidate for governor.[78]

The country is quite hilly in this part, from this place to Columbus. The crops look well.[79]

Monday [September] 28th [1863]

At 7 A.M., [we] came into Columbus [OH]. Here we got our breakfast, which was pork, bread & coffee. Uncle Sam feeds us well on the road. Today passed through London, Dayton, Centerville [OH], Indianapolis. Here we got supper. This is in Indiana.

Tuesday [September] 29th [1863]

This morning we came into Jeffersonville on the Ohio River. We went across on a ferry boat to Louisville, Ky. Both of these places are large cities.

Louisville is the richest place I was ever in. The houses are very large and [there are] plenty of niggers in each. We were cheered but once in this place and that was by a young lady. She waved a flag as we passed by the house. Here we got breakfast. Today [we] passed through Bowling Green, Franklin [KY] and are in Tennessee.

Wednesday [September] 30th [1863]

Last night [we] went through Nashville and out of the state of Tennessee into Alabama. We went on through Stevenson to Bridgeport on the Tennessee River, where we got off from the cars and went into camp.

We are at our journey's end. We rode for 5½ days and now are within about 25 miles of the front, where [William S.] Rosecrans had his great fight.⁸⁰ When I got here I was pretty well worn out with riding. My head felt as though I had been whirled around for half an hour. All the sleep I had was on the cars; and there were from 40 to 20 men in each car and nothing but boards for seats, so there was but little sleeping done.

Now I have been in the states of N.Y., Penn., Md., Ohio, Indiana, Ky., Va., Tenn. & Ala., I have [been] in the cities of Washington, Baltimore, Dayton, Cumberland, Columbus, London, Jeffersonville, Louisville, Indianapolis and Nashville but I was asleep when I went through the last place.

Indiana is the best looking state that we went through.⁸¹

Thursday [October] 1st [1863]

I sleeped well last night and this morning felt pretty well. It has rained all night quite hard. It is warmer here than in Va. It has rained all day and tonight has come off clear.

Friday [October] 2nd [1863]

This morning the sun came up nice and warm. I cleaned my gun and was detailed for picket. I am about 2 miles from camp on an Island that is five miles long and ½ [a mile] across.

Saturday [October] 3rd [1863]

I was released from picket at 7 P.M. and went to camp.

Sun. [October] 4 [1863]

This morning I went to hear the Chaplain of the 33rd Mass. Reg't. His text was "Speak unto the children of Israel to go forward," or that they go forward (I do not know which is right).

It was not much of a sermon but an exhortation for us to work as well for a blessing as we would pray for one. He said, when the time came for us to go forward, we should go with a will to succeed, I expect to conquer, for we were in the right, and the Leader [Abraham Lincoln], we have now is one who has always won. He had got the good will of the soldiers and people by his zeal & patriotism.

Mon. [October] 5 [1863]

There is nothing worthy of notice, today, except that the "new comers" [recruits] had drill in the bayonet exercise. We can not hear any news from the front.[82]

Sat. [October] 10 [1863]

This morning all the Reg't. went ten miles from here but we [Co. E] stayed behind.

Mon. [October] 12 [1863]

This afternoon our company took the cars and went to Anderson 12 miles. This place is on the line between Tenn. & Ala. Last night it rained some.[83]

Tues. [October] 13 [1863]

It has been raining all day.

Wed. [October] 14 [1863]

Last night I was on picket. It rained most all night and we had to either sit or stand up all night.[84]

Wed. [October] 21 [1863]

For a few days past I have been on guard every other day but now I do not have so much to do. Our Reg't. is on the railroad for good. There are three companies here and the Colonel has his quarters here.

My tent is built up with boards and has a fire place. It is 7½ feet wide and 11 [feet] long. There are three of us in it. I never had a better tent. We were four days building it.

But what should happen but that another Reg't. should be sent here to take our place. Our Col. is trying hard to stay but I can not tell with what success.

Fri. [October] 23 [1863]

We are still in the same place. There is some talk of going this afternoon. I can not tell how it will be. I was on picket yesterday and came off this morning.

It rained towards morning and is raining yet. We have rain quite often in these parts.

Gen. [Ulysses S.] Grant passed through here tonight, going to the front and last night Gen. Rosecrans came from the front going north.

Mon. [October] 26 [1863]

Marched, this morning, out of camp at 7 A.M. and went to Bridgeport, 16 miles, which place we got to just after dark. In going to this place, we had to climb a very high mountain. [It was] the worst I ever was on.

Tues. [October] 27 [1863]

We crossed the Tennessee River and marched about 15 miles, towards Chattanooga, where we stopped for the night. The troops, that are here, are from the 11th & 12th Corps with a few western troops. Gens. Hooker and Howard are with us. Hooker is the head man. We are marching for the left wing of [Braxton] Bragg's army.

Wed. [October] 28 [1863]

We continued our march and at about 2 P.M. came to where there were some rebels but we pushed on by them, as they were on the mountain (Lookout). They favored us with a few shells while passing but without any serious damage. While we were in this dangerous place Gen. Hooker rode right out, in plain sight of the rebels. He seemed to [show] but little [concern] for the shells.

The mountain, [which] the rebels are on, is called Lookout [Mountain]. Some of the Reg'ts. lost some men in going by this place. We camped about 3 miles from Chattanooga, where we formed a junction with the main army.

Thurs. [October] 29 [1863]

Last night at 1 A.M. we were woke up by firing and got into line of battle and marched out into the fields. Here we stayed but a few minutes, when the order came to charge up a small but very steep hill, and drive the rebels off. We went up the hill and just at the top the rebels fired and run, taking advantage of that piece of poetry, "He that fights, and runs away Will live to fight another day."[85]

We returned the fire with good effect, killing and wounding about 25. We lost but 6 or 8 men. Our company was very fortunate, for we did not lose any. I think our Brigade killed and wounded about 150 rebels. These figures are only guessed at and may not be right. Our loss in the Reg't. was 2 killed and 4 wounded. These figures are from the Adj. [Campbell Harris Young]. We have built breastworks on this hill and are in a strong place. The rebels have fired a few shell this way today but with no effect. They can not get a good range on us. The fire was returned by our men.[86]

Fri. [October] 30 [1863]

There has been no firing today. Our picket line was put forward 100 rods. Our object, in coming here, was to open this road to Bridgeport; before this we had to draw our supplies 60 miles and it will be but 30 now. The railroad, too, is open now and when we can get it repaired we shall have no trouble about rations.

Sat. [October] 31 [1863]

Today we are to be mustered for pay.[87]

Sun. [November] 1 [1863]

Went to the Corps commissary for some hard tack but I could not get any, unless a commissioned officer was with me. So I went back and got Lieut. [Bishop] True, and then I got them but only half as much as I wanted. I wanted ten lbs. but got but 5 lbs.

Mon. [November] 2 [1863]

All is quiet today, except a few shells flying in the air but they did no harm.

Tues. [November] 3 [1863]

Same as yesterday. One shell came nearer to camp than I like but did no harm.

Fri. [November] 6 [1863]

This morning the enemy threw more shells than common and with good aim. One struck in our camp only 8 feet from the Orderly's tent but it did no harm. It went into the earth 2 or three feet. They shell us to keep us from building breastworks, which we are at all the time, in squads from 20 to a 100 at a time. But the work goes on as ever.

To night I am on picket. The rebel's picket [and] ours are quite near but they have agreed not to fire on each other unless there is an advance made.

Sat. [November] 7 [1863]

This morning we are favored with shells but no harm done. I am in from picket all right.

Sun. [November] 8 [1863]

Most of the men are out chopping today. The woods were quite thick when we came in here but they will soon be down.

Tues. [November] 10 [1863]

Last night we had a battery of artillery brought up. One of the guns was put close to my tent, which I did not like much but they were covered up with brush, so the enemy could not see them. Today we are moving our tents so that they will be out of the way of the guns.

They shell about the same as common from Lookout [Mountain]. Tonight our folks sent a few shells from Chattanooga up to the rebels.[88]

Wednes. [November] 11 [1863]

I am on picket today. The pickets are quite friendly and talk some with us.[89]

Sun. [November] 15 [1863]

This morning I am on camp guard.[90]

Mon. [November] 16 [1863]

The rebels fired four shells this morning that burst over our camp. The pieces went into a tent and another threw dirt into one of the boy's spiders. So you see that there is some danger. When a shell bursts the pieces will go a quarter of a mile and wound very badly. They come with as much force as a bullet does from a gun and when they first strike are hot, so that they both wound and burn.

I hear that Gen. [Robert E.] Lee is to take Gen. [Braxton] Bragg's place, and Gen. [James] Longstreet is to take command in Virginia and Gen. Bragg is going to Mobile.[91] I think, by this, that the rebels are going to do their best in Tennessee.[92]

Tues. [November] 17 [1863]

The enemy have fired but once this way today and then it fell short.

Sun. [November] 22 [1863]

At 1 P.M. left our camp and went to Chattanooga. Which place we got to at dark. Our whole corps is along. We had hard work to get wood enough to cook our food. It has been used up by the soldiers for cooking and keeping warm.

Mon. [November] 23 [1863]

At noon today the enemy was attacked in the center of the army of Gen. [George H.] Thomas, and our corps (Gen. Howard's) was formed on the left and Gen. Hooker [was] on the right opposite Lookout Mountain.[93]

At half past three our corps advanced and drove the enemy about half a mile. The 3rd Div. (Gen. [John White] Geary's) was on the right and the 2nd (our Div.) was on the left and our Reg't. was on the right of the Div.[94]

When we advanced Co. I was put forward as skirmishers and the Reg't. kept 100 yards behind them. In this fight Co. I had both officers wounded and one man [wounded] and Co. F had one [enlisted man] killed.[95]

When we had got on to the line we wanted, we were halted and lay down flat on the ground, while a perfect shower of bullets flew over our heads. Here we stayed until dark and then built breastworks of rails & dirt behind which to lie tomorrow. Our folks have four thirty-two pounders which they have fired some at the enemy.[96]

Tuesday [November] 24 [1863]

There has been very hard fighting all day over to the right. Where we are there has been but little firing. We lost one man in our Co. by name Joseph Sinnott & Co's. A & G lost each one man. Our Reg't. has had ten wounded & one killed.[97]

Wednesday [November] 25 [1863]

This morning out Corps moved to the left & rear of Missionary Ridge, while some of the other troops attacked them in front & on the right. Only a part of our Corps was in this fight & we were lucky enough to be out of it.

Tonight I went out on picket. We were not allowed to build fires. It was very cold. After being out two hours we were permitted to go back of over a hill & build fires to get warm by. At 8 P.M. an officer came round the line & told us that Gen. Grant had taken Missionary Ridge with most of the cannon & that the rebels were retreating. You ought to have heard the boys shout & cheer. I was proud then that I was a soldier. We did not suffer any more for the want of fire; for we each built large fires on our posts.

Thursday [November] 26 [1863]

This morning before light we were in pursuit of the enemy. Our advance guard and their rear guard fought some today. We did not stop until after dark.

Friday [November] 27 [1863]

We marched all day & at dark got to Red Clay Station. There we tore up the track, burned two bridges & depot with 2 cars. This is the railroad that Longstreet has to get his supplies on. We then went back 6 miles & camped at 12 P.M. It rained after dark—hard.

Saturday [November] 28 [1863]

We have today to rest. Tomorrow we have to march again.

Sunday [November] 29 [1863]

This morning we were on our way before it was light and marched until after dark, when we camp in a piece of woods near to Cleveland. I may as well tell here what we have to carry on this march. When we went into the fight we left our knapsacks & all that was in them except a overcoat and rubber blankets and guns with 60 rounds of cartridge.

We have to build up large fires in order to keep warm and sleep any at night—as it freezes hard every night.

We are near the road that leads to Knoxville, Tenn. The Qr. [Quarter Master Jacob S. Galentine] takes all of the cattle and horses that he meets with and corn or wheat.[98] We live almost all together on the country.[99]

Monday [November] 30th [1863]

This morning we started at 8 a.m. and marched till noon when we came to Charleston. Here we meet some rebs but they would not stay to see us. We captured some flour and meal with bacon and salt. The rebels left it in their hurry to get away. There is a river here by the name of the Hiwassee.[100]

Tuesday [December 1, 1863]

Today we went to Athens [GA] where we stayed for the night. It is 16 miles from the camp of last night to this place.[101]

Wednesday [December] 2 [1863]

Today we went to Philadelphia. We started before light & did not get into camp before dark. The last two days have been quite cold.

Thursday [December] 3 [1863]

This morning we were off by 5 A.M. & went about 5 miles to the Tennessee River where we rested until [Saturday].[102]

Saturday [December] 5 [1863]

When we left at 2 A.M. & went 6 miles up the river to cross on a bridge which we made out of wagons & planks. We marched to the town of Louisville—15 miles from Knoxville—where we heard that Gen. Burnside had defeated the Rebels.

Sunday [December] 6 [1863]

I went to church today in Louisville & heard a good Sermon from the Chaplain of the 55th New Jersey Regiment. The text was II Cor. IV.5 "We preach not ourselves, but Christ Jesus the Lord." This is the first time I have been in a church since I left home.

Monday [December] 7 [1863]

This morning we started back for Chattanooga, I suppose. Crossed the river & camped just after dark.

Tuesday [December] 8 [1863]

Today we got to Philadelphia. It rained some which made it hard walking & we work on the railroad track.

Wednesday [December] 9 [1863]

This day we came to Athens at 5 P.M. & went on picket.

Thursday [December] 10 [1863]

[We] are here yet & are drawing rations of meal & flour. I have not been relieved yet from picket.

Friday [December] 11 [1863]

Last night I came in from picket & had a good sleep at night. Today I have nothing to do but rest.[103]

Saturday [December] 12 [1863]

This morning we left at day light & marched 2 miles beyond Charleston where we camped for the night. Tonight it rained quite hard but stopped before morning. Distance 13 miles.

Sunday [December] 13 [1863]

Went to Cleveland nine miles & stayed 2 days. Here our supply house (wagoner) met us with rations. [We] are glad enough to get them for they are the first after 18 days. During this time I have drank corn coffee. I like it quite well.[104]

Wednesday [December] 16 [1863]

This morning we left Cleveland for Chattanooga and went half way which is fifteen miles & camped. At 5 P.M. were within 2 miles of camp which we did not reach until 9 P.M.—2 miles in 4 hours! Most of this time there was a hard rain. These 2 miles were through a pass in the mountains where the Chickamauga Creek runs. A part of the way, we went one at a time through the mud over our shoes. It was as dark as a dungeon & when we got into camp it was so rainy that I did not cook any supper but went over and crawled into a barn at 12½ A.M. & slept until 4 o'clock when I went back to camp & got breakfast.

Thursday [December] 17 [1863]

Today we got back to our old camp which we left Nov. 22nd. I am almost used up. I am lame sure & covered with dirt & black as an Indian. I wore out a new pair of shoes on this march.

We covered about 250 miles. From Chattanooga to Knoxville by rail is 250 miles. We went with 15 miles of it & that on a road more crooked than the railroad.

I found my knapsack & all therein except an old tent which is but little loss. I am glad to get through it all with a whole skin.

I think our campaigning is over until the Spring. When, I suppose, we shall have to go at it again. We expect to move our camp over near to Gen. Hooker's headquarters & build quarters for the winter. It is quite cold & I have nothing to put on my hands[105] & cannot buy any mittens or gloves here for love or money.

Wednesday [December] 23d [1863]

Our Brigade is to work on the road to day.[106]

Friday [December] 25th [1863]

Today is Christmas but for all that we are to work on our new camp. There are six in my tent with me. My Christmas dinner is about half as much hard tack and bacon as a man can eat but to night we draw rations. I can get all I wish from Lieut. True simply by asking him for an order on the commissary for rations, but to day the commissary had no hard tack. Last Christmas I was in the army but had a good dinner, today I had a very poor one.[107]

Saturday [December] 26th [1863]

It rains some today—working on the camp.

Sunday [December] 27th [1863]

It rains quite hard to day. We worked some on our camp but the rain drove us off. I think it wrong but cannot help it. We were ordered to work and have to do it. I am writing this by candle-light.[108]

FOOTNOTES

1. Discharged with a disability:
    January 3 — Joseph Rolls (Co. A).
    January 7 — Cpl. John Galbraith, Jr. (Co. F), Philip Bertram (Co. I).
    January 8 — Hiram Weaver (Co. H).
    January 15 — Reuben Fish (Co. A).
    January 17 — Cpl. Harrison Broughton (Co. H).
    January 18 — Henry McCullough (Co. F).
    January 19 — Chester Gould (Co. C) and Charles Bassett, John Lester (both Co. E).
    January 25 — Worthington Luce (Co. B).
   Discharged: January 8 — Horace Brownell (Co. D).
    January 11 — 2nd Lt. John W. Webster (Co. A).
    January 12 — Sylvester Summers (Co. C) and Sgt. Covil Olney (Co. D).
    January 13 — Cpt. Ezra Jeffres — (Co. H).
    January 18 — 2nd Lt. Nicholas Mundy (Co. B) and Coryden Card (Co. D), 2nd Lt. Charles H. Wisner (Co. F), 1st Lt. Edward Madden — (Co. H).
    January 19 — Harvey Gibbs (Co. C) and Asst. Surg. Charles F. Warner — reinstated — no date.
    January 22 — Cpt. Augustus Harrington (Co, D).
   Deserted: January 13 — James H. Roberts (Co. I).
    January 16 — Henry Denison (Co. C).
    January 22 — Herbert Bishop and Lewis Sharow (both Co. G).
   Transferred to VRC (Veteran Reserve Corps):
    January 1 — Norman Hamilton (Co. C).
   Died of disease: January 2 — James H. Wheelor (Co. K) from fever.
    January 12 — Thomas Clinton (Co. D).

2. Discharged with a disability:
    January 26 — Barney Williams (Co. F).
    January 28 — Charles Quick (Co. B).
    January 29 — Charles Barnard (Co. G).
   Died of Wounds:
    January 27 — Cpl. Robert Dow (Co. E).
    January 30 — Charles Carpenter (Co. E) from an accidental wound.
   Discharged: January 29 — Henry F. Scott (Co. K).
    January 31 — John W. Sickles (Co. F).
   Died: January 30 — Jerome Henry (Co. I).

3. The infamous "Mud March" of January 1863 left more than a reasonable share of men in the 136th New York unfit for further service. By February 4, five more soldiers received medical discharges:
    February 1 — 1st Lt. Russell Dudley (Co. D).
    February 2 — Joel M. Potter (Co. H).
    February 3 — Joseph Van Valkenburgh (Co. C).
    February 4 — Florus Dieffenbacher (Co. G) and James Welstead (Co. I).

TAGO, Record Group 94, Muster Rolls, Returns, Regimental Papers, Volunteer Organizations of the Civil War, Box 3295, NY 136th Inf., Return for January, 1863.

4. Died: John Haskins (Co. A).

5. Discharged with disability:
   February 6 — Christopher Allen (Co. A).
   February 8 — Dennis Gardner (Co. A).
   February 10 — Joseph W. McKee (Co. K).
   February 11 — William Dart (Co. F).
   Died from disease: February 7 — Eliphalet Slate (Co. F).
   Discharged: February 7 — William Albro and Zedrick Barnes (both Co. D).
   February 10 — James Skuse (Co. F).

6. Discharged with a disability: Andrew J. Simons (Co. E).
   February 17 — Charles R. Randall and Jonas Dunbar (both Co. H).
   Died of disease: February 17 — William Parker (Co. F).

   Joseph Hooker, major general, U.S.A., commanded the Army of the Potomac.
   Franz Sigel, major general, U.S.A., had no actual command at this time. He was just another general without any real troops to order about.
   (Warner, *Generals in Blue*, 1959, 233-235, 447-448)

7. Died: February 19 — James French (Co. F).
   February 20 — Samuel Young (Co. I).
   February 22 — William Z. Williams (Co. F).
   Transferred to the VRC: February 25 — Daniel Corbin (Co. K).
   Discharged: February 18 — Gilbert L. Lewis (Co. I).
   February 22 — Patrick McGuire (Co. G).
   Discharged with disabilities:
   February 19 — Musician Thomas Cole (Co. B).
   February 21 — Griffin Camp (Co. D).
   February 22 — Edwin Pasco (Co. K).
   February 23 — Andrew Orcutt (Co. E) and Jonas Squrbier (Co. I).
   February 25 — Martin Brenan (Co. C).
   February 26 — James Graham (Co. F).
   February 27 — John Baker (Co. H) and Abram Teetsworth (Co. I).
   February 28 — William Holmes and Alexander Gardner (both Co. A).

8. March showed no marked improvement over the preceding months in relation to medical discharges or deaths from disease.
   Discharged with disabilities:
   March 1 — Patrick Reilly and Abner Robinson (both Co. F).
   March 3 — John H. Rogers (Co. B), Cpl. Neil Callaghan (Co. D), and Michael Grely (Co. F).
   March 5 — Jacob Gatz (Co. H).
   March 6 — James May and Cpl. William Polen (Co. I).
   March 7 — Samuel Bowen (Co. H).
   Discharged: March 3 — Oliver Dewey (Co. D)
   Died of disease: March 4 — James Dunn (Co. G) from chronic diarrhea.
   March 6 — William Millhollen (Co. K) from chronic diarrhea.
   Died: March 7 — Musician Orrin Locke (Co. C).

TAGO, Record Group 94, Muster Rolls, Returns, Regimental Papers, Volunteer Organizations of the Civil War, Box 3295, NY 136th Inf., Return for February, 1863.

9. Discharged with a disability: Joel Johnson (Co. I).

10. The entire regiment needed a good scrubbing. Typhus, resulting from lice infestation, appeared within the ranks.
    Died from disease: March 8 — Robert Burke (Co. H) from typhus.
    Discharged with a disability:
          March 8 — Musician James Phillips (Co. E).
          March 9 — Horace Wing (Co. I).
    Discharged: March 10 — Ira Ackerman (Co. D).
          March 11 — 1st Lt. George Bass (Co. K).

    Private Charles H. Harrington received his commission in the mail to the 2nd lieutenancy of Company D with orders to report to the regiment on March 5. He deserted in Washington, DC and escaped custody, never to be seen again.

11. Discharged with a disability: March 12 — Aaron Hotchkiss (Co. K).
    Discharged: March 12 — John Cummings (Co. D).
          March 13 — Cpt. Henry Jenks (Co. E).
    Died of disease: March 13 — Patrick Ryan (Co. H) from typhus.

12. Died of disease: March 15 — Zebulon Doty (Co. G) from chronic diarrhea.
    Discharged with disabilities:
          March 16 — Norman Gibbs (Co. I).
          March 18 — William Lincoln (Co. D) and Cpt. Sidney Ward (Co. G).
    Deserted: March 18 — John Curtis (Co. D).

13. Discharged with a disability: Elijah Hall (Co. A).
    Deserted: DeWitt Heminway (Co. E) while on furlough.

14. Adolph Wilhelm August Friedrich, Baron von Steinwehr, brigadier general, U.S.A., commanded the Second Division of the XI Corps, Army of the Potomac. (Warner, *Generals in Blue*, 1959, 530-531)

15. Died from disease: James McBallard (Co. A) from lung congestion.

16. Discharged with disability:
          March 24 — Myron Bow (Co. G).
          March 28 — Cpl. Washington Hatch and Henry H. Wright (Co. A), Allen C. Wallace (Co. C), Cpl. Frank Johnson (Co. E), and Jacob Landen (Co. G).
          March 30 — Reuben Gray (Co. E).
          March 31 — Delos Hoffman (Co. A).
    Died from disease: March 24 — Daniel Johnson (Co. G) from consumption.

    As usual disabilities, death, and desertion accounted for most of the regiment's attrition. By the beginning of April the 136th New York carried 774 officers and enlisted men. 6 officers were on leave. 34 enlisted men had been sent to duty away from the ranks. 12 had legitimate leave of absences. 21 remained absent without leave. 99 were sick and 2 were under arrest. 22% of the total strength were not present for duty.

TAGO, Record Group 94, Muster Rolls, Returns, Regimental Papers, Volunteer Organizations of the Civil War, Box 3295, NY 136th Inf., Return for March, 1863.

April, with its milder weather brought some much needed relief from the persistent drain in manpower. Between April 1 and the entry on April 10, only two men.

Discharged with disabilities:
April 2 — Benjamin Clow (Co. E).
April 4 — William G. Truesdell (Co. A).
Deserted: George J. Smith (Co. K).

17. The boy was Thomas, whom the President nicknamed "Tad" for "Tadpole." He was the Lincolns' only surviving child and as a result was terribly spoiled.

18. Oliver Otis Howard, major general, U.S.A., commanded the much maligned XI Corps at Chancellorsville and Gettysburg.
(Warner, *Generals in Blue*, 1959, 237-239)

19. Sick (No further record): Edwin Hamilton (Co. I).
Discharged with disabilities:
April 11 — James Culvor (Co. B).
April 13 — Frank Flint (Co. D).
April 15 — Reuben Lane (Co. E).
April 16 — Musician Joel M. W. Smith (Co. B).
April 20 — Cpl. George Dippy (Co. B) and Joseph Barnhart (Co. I).
April 22 — Harvey Melvin (Co. D).
Discharged: April 15 — Henry Chamberlin (Co. D).
Deserted: April 21 — Joseph Macauley (Co. E) while on furlough.

20. Discharged with disability: Daniel McCarthy (Co. K).

21. Transferred to the VRC: Henry Havens (Co. I).

The month of April had been a merciful one. The regiment lost only 14 men that month, bringing the enrollment to 747 of whom only 603 reported for duty with the regiment.
TAGO, Record Group 94, Muster Rolls, Returns, Regimental Papers, Volunteer Organizations of the Civil War, Box 3295, NY 136th Inf., Return for April, 1863.

22. Killed in action: Addison Howell (Co. K).
Missing in action: Albert G. Sharples (Co. F).

While acting as the rearguard on May 3, the regiment suffered one more casualty. George Moore (Co. C) was wounded. Three other men were reported as missing and a second man was said to be killed. In all likelihood, Albert Sharples was the man listed as dead and the three men who deserted after the battle showed up as captured or missing in the *Official Records*.
(Phisterer, IV, 1912, 3582)

23. The 136th New York lost 2 men killed, 1 man wounded and 3 missing for an aggregate of 6 casualties.
(Phisterer, IV, 1912, 3582)

24. Deserted: Irving Lindsley (Co. C).

25. Deserted: William Hill (Co. G).

26. Resigned: Cpt. Wells Hendershott (Co. D).
    An officer could "resign" from the service, which is another way of saying he was discharged. Officers, as a rule, "resigned" just as they "enrolled" and enlisted men "enlisted."
    Deserted: May 13 — Charles Powers (Co. K).
    Discharged with disabilities:
        May 14 — John Kellogg (Co. K).
        May 15 — Cpt. Kidder M. Scott (Co. H).
        May 16 — Benjamin Sweeten (Co. E).
        May 27 — Charles Coffee (Co. E).
    Discharged: May 14 — 1st Lt. Emerson Hoyt (Co. C).
        May 21 — Maj. Davis Hartshorn.

27. The best month to date in regard to casualties, the 136th New York dropped off by 11 men, bringing its book strength to 735. 81% (599 men) could report for duty.
    June, which proved to be the healthiest one for the regiment to date did not start off well. On June 2, First Sergeant Harrison Barber (Co. K), the highest ranking enlisted man to desert thus far in the war, failed to report back from furlough. On the same day, Harlow McCray (Co. H) was discharged with a disability.
    TAGO, Record Group 94, Muster Rolls, Returns, Regimental Papers, Volunteer Organizations of the Civil War, Box 3295, NY 136th Inf., Return for May, 1863.

28. Resigned: June 6 — Cpt. Almon Hoyt (Co. C).
    Discharged with a disability: June 6 — Willard Joslyn (Co. H).

29. Deserted: James Elwell (Co. H) from the hospital.

30. Deserted: John Quincy Adams (Co. F).

31. Deserted: John Kelly (Co. F) and Marshal Joslyn (Co. H) at Emmitsburg.
    Desertion accounted for 50% of the regiment's 8 casualties during June.
    The regiment mustered 556 men present for duty. 23% of the officers and men were absent but still on the rolls. Not counting the 6 officers who reported either sick, on detached service, or on leave, 161 enlisted personnel did not report for duty: 43 detached; 9 AWOL; 107 sick; 2 under arrest.
    TAGO, Record Group 94, Muster Rolls, Returns, Regimental Papers, Volunteer Organizations of the Civil War, Box 3295, NY 136th Inf., Return for June, 1863.

32. According to First Sergeant Lucien A. Smith (Co. G) the regiment was deployed in line of battle perpendicular to the road [Steinwehr Avenue] which led into the cemetery with one of the flanks near the gate. Later in the day, the regiment moved down into the road paralleling the front of the cemetery.
    After dark, the regiment moved back to the cemetery road and lay down in open ranks to the left of the road further to the front of its original position. Lying under rather heavy fire to which it did not respond, the regiment shifted back to the road east of the cemetery with the entrance on its right. It spent the night in that position. The regimental adjutant, who did not keep very

accurate records, recorded three casualties of whom only one, William Hewitt (Co. F) appears as wounded. The remaining two known casualties were Levi G. Smith and Charles Jones (both Co. K), both of whom deserted on this day. The wounded man in Company E has not been recorded.

Ken Bandy and Florence Freeland, (comp.), *The Gettysburg Papers*, Vol. III, (Dayton, OH: Morningside Bookshop, 1978), 299-300.

33. Company G ended up on the skirmish line in the morning, well in advance to the front of the regiment. Later on, as the skirmishing continued, another company came to assist Company G. During the change in formation, an officer and an enlisted man rescued Corporal Lucien J. Smith (Co. G) from an exposed position between the lines. Sergeant Lucien A. Smith (Co. G) stopped the stretcher party as it carried Lucien J. Smith to the rear and said he was sorry for the corporal. The corporal told his sergeant, "It is all over with me, but you little know what you have to go through."

    For the known casualties of the 136th New York refer to Appendix A.
    (Bandy and Freeland, III, 1978, 302)

34. James Lavery enlisted in Lima on July 30, 1862 when he was 39 years old. He lost the sight in his right eye but was not injured severely enough to leave the service. He was transferred to the Veteran Reserve Corps and died in 1874.

    Gettysburg cost the regiment 109 effectives: 17 men killed, 10 rank and file mortally wounded, 1 officer and 78 enlisted men wounded and 1 officer and 2 soldiers missing.
    (Smith 1881, 484)
    (*A Record of the Commissioned Officers.....*, , III, n.d., 697)
    (Phisterer, IV, 1912, 3582)

35. Richard Youells (Co. C) died from his wounds which he received the day before. John Stowell (Co. H) also perished from his injuries.

    The Confederates wounded Baldess Foote (Co. B) and Matthaus Vollmer (Co. D) during the mopping up of the battlefield. Vollmer never returned to the regiment for active duty again.

36. Frederick Phisterer, Vol. IV, p. 3592.

    Bishop H. True, age 19, enrolled on August 11, 1862 at Lima to serve 3 years in Company E, 136th New York; mustered in as the First Sergeant of Company E on September 25, 1862; on March 12, 1863, mustered in as Second Lieutenant; mustered out with the company on June 13, 1865, near Washington, DC; commissioned Second Lieutenant on March 12, 1863, vice Seth P. Buell, promoted.

    James H. Smith, *1687 History of Livingston County, New York*, D. Mason & Co., Syracuse, NY, 1881, p. 484.

    Bishop True died before 1881. He would have been 38 years old.

37. Deserted: Musician George Cole and Thomas Easton (both Co. B), Elisha Bracey and Thomas Nelson (both Co. D), Manilus Gay (Co. E), and Barney Teague (Co. G).

38. Deserted: Cpl. Michael Touhil and James A. Yencer (both Co. F).

39. Died from wounds: Henry Limerick (Co. F).

40. Resigned: Cpt. Seth Buell (Co. E).

41. Deserted: Isaac Lockwood (Co. B).

42. Transferred to VRC: Covel Cowley (Co. E).

43. Died from wounds: Daniel V. Hull (Co. G).

44. Discharged: John McCoy (Co. C).

45. Deserted: James Henry (Co. C).

46. George E. Torrey, age 24, enlisted on August 11, 1862 at Lima, New York to serve 3 years; mustered in as a Private in Company G, 130th New York; Sergeant on September 3, 1862; promoted to First Sergeant on August 12, 1863. On November 1, 1864, he mustered in as Second Lieutenant; mustered out with his company on June 30, 1865 at Cloud's Mill, Virginia; commissioned as Second Lieutenant on January 31, 1865, with the rank from October 31, 1864 vice Justus F. Coy, promoted. The regimental history dates his appointment to the Second Lieutenancy as February 9, 1865.
    (Phisterer, II, 1912, 1160)

    (*Regimental History of the First New York Dragoons*, 1865, 26)

47. Guilford Wiley Wells enrolled on August 20, 1862 at Portage to serve 3 years in Company G, 130th New York; mustered in as Second Lieutenant on August 20, 1862 and as First Lieutenant on October 10, 1862; mustered in as Captain on August 12, 1863; wounded in action at Trevilian Station, Virginia, on June 12, 1864 which forced him to resign because of disability on September 5, 1864; discharge revoked and was reinstated on September 14, 1864. His wounds eventually forced his discharge on February 10, 1865. On March 13, 1865 he received a brevet as a Lieutenant Colonel of Volunteers; commissioned Second Lieutenant November 1, 1862 with the rank from August 20, 1862, original; commissioned First Lieutenant November 24, 1862 with rank from October 9, 1862, vice Charles L. Brundage, promoted, and as Captain on August 21, 1863, with rank from August 12, 1863, also, vice Brundage, promoted.
    (Phisterer, II, 1912, 1161)

48. George Henry Chappell was born in Avon in 1838. He enlisted on May 7, 1861 in the 27th New York in Company G when he was 23 years old. Serving the entire war, he came home to Avon, where he died in either 1866 or 1867.
    (Smith 1881, 480)

    (*Register of Commissioned Officers*, I, n.d., 622)

49. Charles Harding, age 18, enlisted August 9, 1862 at Mount Morris; mustered in as a Private in Company B, 130th New York to serve 3 years; promoted to Corporal July 18, 1864; to Sergeant, March 20, 1865; mustered out with company, June 30, 1865 at Clouds Mills, VA.
    (*Regimental History of the First New York Dragoons*, 1865, 30)

    (*Annual Report of the Adjutant General of the State of New York*, II, 1896, 76)

50. Henry Gale, age 22, enlisted on August 4, 1862, at Dansville, New York to serve 3 years in Company B of the 130th New York; mustered in as a private on August 9, 1862 and was promoted to Sergeant then to Sergeant-Major by

March 1, 1863. On May 11, 1863 he became the company's Second Lieutenant. On October 30, 1863 he mustered in as the company's First Lieutenant. Wounded in action on May 8, 1864, he received a discharge for disability on September 7, 1864. He was breveted a Captain of New York Volunteers then he received a brevet to Captain of U.S. Volunteers as of March 13, 1865. He was commissioned Second Lieutenant May 27, 1863 with rank from May 11, 1863, vice Gilbert E. Bursley, resigned. His commission to First Lieutenant dates from August 21, 1863 with the rank from August 1, 1863, vice Samuel Culbertson, promoted.
(Phisterer, II, 1912, 1155-1156)

51. Died from wounds: Cpl. Lucien J. Smith (Co. G).

Charles House, age 26, enlisted on August 6, 1862 at Leicester, New York to serve 3 years; mustered in as a Private, Company B, 130th New York on August 9, 1862; mustered out with company on June 30, 1865 at Clouds Mills, Virginia.
(*Regimental History of the First New York Dragoons*, 1865, 31)
(*Adjutant General's Report of the State of New York*, III, 1896, 88)

52. Deserted: Robert Jackson and Harrison Lyon (both Co. C).
Captured and released: Ira D. Peckham (Co. K).
Hospitalized with no further record: John D. Sortore (Co. K).

53. Died from disease: Joshua Gage (Co. B) from typhus.

54. Deserted: John Johnson (Co. D) and Morgan Mayhew (Co. H).

55. Discharged with a disability: Thomas Levers (Co. B).

56. Wounded in action: George Snyder (Co. K).

57. Died from wounds: Zack Barber (Co. K).

58. Discharged with a disability: 2nd Lt. John Lottridge.

By the end of July, the 136th New York had approximately 641 men on the books. Desertions (16) and killed in action (14) accounted for the largest percentage of casualties. 34% of that number (218 people) did not report for duty. 7 officers were down, either detached from the regiment or ill. The number of enlisted men on duty away from the regiment numbered an all time high of 54 men. 6 were AWOL and 151 reported sick.
TAGO, Record Group 94, Muster Rolls, Returns, Regimental Papers, Volunteer Organizations of the Civil War, Box 3295, NY 136th Inf., Return for July, 1863.

59. The man who died did not get recorded by the adjutant or his 1st Sergeant.
Died from wounds: George Mosher (Co. H) at Camp Letterman.
Transferred to the VRC: Timothy Phelan (Co. F).

60. Deserted: August 12 — Edward McGuire (Co. E).
Died from wounds: August 13 — John Folmsbee (Co. G).

61. Daniel Foster, Chaplain, Residence, Newburyport, Mass., clergyman. He was commissioned and mustered August 13, 1862; discharged to accept a com-

mission in U.S. Colored Troops on November 16, 1863.
The Adjutant General, *Massachusetts Soldiers, Sailors, And Marines in the Civil War*, Vol. III, (Norwood, Mass: Norwood Press, 1932), 538.

62. Resigned: 1st Lt. H. Edward Van Zandt (Co. A).

63. Discharged: James Harrison Moore (Co. D).

64. Discharged for wounds: Cpl. Lucius Bradley (Co. B).

65. Discharged with a disability: Robert Clark (Co. B).

66. Discharged: William Harris (Co. B).
Paroled: August 28 — Cpl. John Hayen (Co. G).

67. Died from wounds: Simeon Ikins (Co. K).
Discharged with a disability: George W. Wescott (Co. I).

68. The First New York Dragoons were also designated the 19th New York Cavalry.

69. Book strength for the regiment stood at 635 officers and men, of whom only 425 reported for duty.
TAGO, Record Group 94, Muster Rolls, Returns, Regimental Papers, Volunteer Organizations of the Civil War, Box 3295, NY 136th Inf., Return for August, 1863.

70. Transferred to the VRC: September 1 — Clark Austin (Co. H).
Discharged with a disability: September 3 — Thomas Wright (Co. A).

71. Discharged with a disability: Cpl. Delos Billings (Co. K).

72. Transferred to the VRC: September 6 — Ephraim E. Tiffany (Co. E).

73. Discharged with a disability: Stephen Bulson (Co. K).

74. Transferred to the VRC: September 12 — Cpt. Dwight Ferris (Co. A).
Discharged for disabilities:
September 12 — Corporal Faulkner Dorr (Co. B) and
John Smith (Co. H).

75. Transferred to the VRC: September 16 — Joseph Finch (Co. A).
Deserted: September 17 — John McGuire (Co. E).

76. Died: Andrew Brown (Co. A).

77. Killed in an accident: Cpl. Martin Quigley (Co. C) died en route when he fell between two of the moving railroad cars.

78. John Brough won the election and served as Governor of Ohio from 1864-1865. (Johnson and Buel, I, 6)

79. Deserted: James Compton (Co. I).

80. William Starke Rosecrans, major general, U.S.A., commanded the Army of

the Cumberland until he was defeated at Chickamauga, Georgia on September 19-20, 1863. U.S. Grant relieved him of command on October 19, 1863. (Warner, *Generals in Blue*, 1959, 410-411)

81. Transferred to the VRC: Sgt. Samuel W. Wilson (Co. G).
    The official regimental strength stood at 621 officers and men of whom only 415 could report for duty.
    TAGO, Record Group 94, Muster Rolls, Returns, Regimental Papers, Volunteer Organizations of the Civil War, Box 3295, NY 136th Inf., Return for September, 1863.

82. Discharged: October 7 — Eli Slack (Co. D).

83. Discharged with a disability: Sgt. Daniel Jincks (Co. D).

84. Discharged with a disability: October 16 — George Moore (Co. C).

85. (Doty 1905, 475-476)
    The Official Records of the War of the Rebellion, Vol. XXXI, part 1, 105-107.

86. In the Battle of Wauhatchie, TN, three regiments from Colonel Orland Smith's brigade, made a midnight assault up an extremely high hill against a superior Confederate force. With orders to use the bayonet only, the three regiments, which numbered less than 700 officers and men, drove an estimated 1,800 Confederates in McIver Law's brigade from the crest.
    The 33rd Massachusetts, with seven companies (about 230 present), held the center. The 73rd Ohio held the right of the line. After detaching Companies H and K to a hill north of the Confederate position, Colonel James Wood, Jr. moved the rest of his regiment to the right and charged up the hill to the support of the two regiments already engaged. Wood estimated the hill to be about 180 yards at a 45 degree angle from the base to the top, with a 6 foot wide crest. His regiment fired one volley into the backs of the fleeing Confederates. The New Yorkers captured 5 Confederates and 40 weapons. The 33rd Massachusetts captured 2 Confederate officers and 39 enlisted men with their weapons and entrenching tools.
    According to the regimental outline in Phisterer, the 136th New York did lose 2 men killed, 1 man mortally wounded and two others non-fatally wounded. The two dead men were Hermann Gardner (Co. A) and Nicholas Gurgen (Co. B). Of the remaining three men — Sergeant V. Bemis Coleman (Co. A), Corporal William Huggins (Co. F), and Alexander R. Russell (Co. F) — Russell's injury was fatal. William Doerflinger (Co. I) parted company with the regiment to go with the Veteran Reserve Corps.

87. Chapin J. Metcalf (D Co.) deserted. His departure left the 136th New York with 616 people on its rolls. Of that number 67% (414 officers and men) stayed within the regiment.
    TAGO, Record Group 94, Muster Rolls, Returns, Regimental Papers, Volunteer Organizations of the Civil War, Box 3295, NY 136th Inf., Return for October, 1863.

88. Died: Thomas Watson (Co. I)

89. Died from wounds: Alexander Russell (Co. F).

90. Transferred to the VRC: Corporal Monroe Annis and James Briggs, and George Bristol (all Co. C), and Robers Lawton (Co. H).

91. Robert E. Lee commanded the Army of Northern Virginia, C.S.A.
    Braxton Bragg, general, C.S.A., commanded the Army of Tennessee at Chickamauga, then the Confederate Army at Chattanooga.
    James Longstreet, lieutenant general, C.S.A., commanded the First Corps, Army of Northern Virginia and was sent south to assist the Confederate forces at Chickamauga, Georgia and Knoxville, Tennessee.
    (Ezra Warner, *Generals in Gray*, 1959, 179-183, 30-31, and 192-193)

92. Transferred to the VRC: Gilbert Rulapaugh (Co. F).

93. George Henry Thomas, major general, U.S.A., had command of the Army of the Cumberland at Chattanooga. Oliver O. Howard had the XI Corps and Joseph Hooker commanded selected divisions of the IV, XII, XIV, and XV Corps.
    (Warner, *Generals in Blue*, 1959, 500-502)

94. John White Geary, brigadier general, U.S.A., was the commander of the Second Division, XII Corps.
    (Warner, *Generals in Blue*, 1959, 169-170)

95. McMahon erred. Company F and Company I each had one officer wounded.
    Robert F. Bullard, age 28, enlisted on August 28, 1862 at Conesus, New York, to serve 3 years; mustered in as First Sergeant of Company I, 136th New York on September 25, 1862 and then as Second Lieutenant on January 17, 1863; wounded in action on November 23, 1863, he was discharged for disability from his wounds on July 5, 1864; commissioned Second Lieutenant on March 12, 1863 with the rank from January 16, 1863, vice George W. Reed, resigned.
    Charles F. Tresser, age 37, enlisted on August 22, 1862 at Mt. Morris, New York; mustered in as Sergeant, Company F, 136th New York on September 25, 1862; mustered in as Second Lieutenant on March 1, 1863 and as First Lieutenant, Company C, on July 4, 1863; wounded in action on November 23, 1863 at Chattanooga, TN; he died from his wounds on December 16, 1863; commissioned Second Lieutenant March 12, 1863 with rank from January 18, 1863, vice Charles H. Wisner, resigned; commissioned First Lieutenant on July 23, 1863 with the rank from May 14, 1863, vice J. Emerson Hoyt, resigned.
    (Phisterer, IV, 1912, 3582, 3586, and 3592)

    According to the casualty reports the 136th New York had 1 man killed (Co. F), 2 officers (Cos. I and F), and 8 enlisted men wounded for a total of 11.
    Phisterer reported 1 enlisted man killed, 1 enlisted man mortally wounded, and 1 officer mortally wounded, and 8 enlisted men wounded.
    (*OR*, XXXI, part 2, 82 and 378)

96. Company I had one officer hit — 2nd Lieutenant Robert Bullard with a flesh wound in the leg. Company C accounted for the other injured officer — 1st Lieutenant Charles Tresser. The three enlisted casualties were Ambrose Yencer (Co. F), who was killed, and Johnathan Britton (Co. C) and William Sorg (Co. I), both of whom were wounded.

97. The 136th lost 11 soldiers at Missionary Ridge. 1 man was killed outright. 1 officer and 1 soldier died from their wounds and 8 men were wounded. McMahon's tabulation of the casualties for November 23-27 agrees with the *Official Records.*
(Phisterer, IV, 1912, 3582)

    Joseph Sinnott (Co. E), who recovered from his minor wound, did not get mentioned among the wounded in the regimental roster. Corporal Rinaldo Griswold was the injured man in Company G. Griswold, according to the regimental roster was wounded on the 29th at Missionary Ridge. The date is in error. He was hit on the 23rd. 1st Sergeant Isaac Kruson (Co. A) was the other casualty with a severe injury to his right hip.
    TAGO, Record Group 94, Descriptive Rolls, Volunteer Organizations of the Civil War, NY 136th Inf., p. 42-43.

98. Jacob S. Galentine, age 28, enlisted on September 6, 1862 at Portage to serve 3 years. He mustered in as a Private in Company I, 136th New York on September 25, 1862. Prior to April 10, 1863 he was promoted to Commissary-Sergeant. He mustered in as First Lieutenant and Quartermaster as of January 23, 1863. He was discharged June 13, 1865 at Rochester, New York. He received his commission to First Lieutenant and Quartermaster on April 24, 1863 with the rank from January 23, 1863, vice Levi R. Vincent, declined.
(Phisterer, IV, 1912, 3588)

99. Discharged: Levi T. Skinner (Co. E) and William H. Porst (Co. I).

100. The regiment now counted approximately 626 men, 231 of whom (37%) could not report for duty. 11 officers were absent: 4 detached; 1 on leave; 1 AWOL; 5 sick. 72 men were on detached service, the highest number to date. 4 were on leave without permission. 143 were sick and 1 was under arrest.
    TAGO, Record Group 94, Muster Rolls, Returns, Regimental Papers, Volunteer Organizations of the Civil War, Box 3295, NY 136th Inf., Return for November, 1863.

101. Transferred to the VRC: William H. H. Taylor (Co. A).

102. Discharged for wounds: Sgt. John Boyd, Jr. (Co. H).

103. Died: Edwin Winans (Co. G).

104. Died of disease: Nathaniel Conger (Co. H) from chronic diarrhea.

105. Discharged for wounds: December 18 — Henry Orr (Co. H).

106. Died from wounds: 1st Lt. Charles F. Tresser (Co. C).

107. Died of disease: John Bristol (Co. B) died from severe diarrhea.
Died from wounds: Nicholas Connor (Co. E).

108. After fifteen months of Federal service the 136th New York had lost about 324 officers and men. 38% (120 men) were discharged with disabilities. 17% (55 men) deserted. 14% (46 men) received discharges for unstated reasons. 8% (27 men) died from disease. 6% (19 men) died from unstated causes. 6% (19 men) were killed in action. 5% (16 men) went into the Veteran Reserve

Corps. 4% (13 men) died from their wounds. 1% (6 men) were reported missing in action. 3 men just disappeared from the rolls and were never heard from again. The regiment counted 620 men on the books of whom 32% (199 officers and men) could not serve with the regiment in the field.

In contrast with the roster's numbers, the regiment actually lost about 349 men by December 1863.

Discharged with a disability: James Hall (Co. G).
Died: December 29 — John V. Plants (Co. A).

TAGO, Record Group 94, Muster Rolls, Returns, Regimental Papers, Volunteer Organizations of the Civil War, Box 3295, NY 136th Inf., Return for December, 1863.

Chapter Four

1864

Jan 1st Friday [1864]

Went to work on the road, but did not work any. It was too cold to work.

Saturday [January] 2nd [1864]

We moved into our new camp today.[1]

Sunday [January] 10th [1864]

This is the first Sunday that I have been at liberty for some time. The day is somewhat cold.[2]

Sunday [January] 24th [1864]

For the last week we have had very warm weather for winter. It has been almost an Indian Summer and today is as warm as ever.

Wednesday [January] 27th [1864]

The weather continues very warm and the boys sit out doors with their coats off. I sweat quite hard while sitting in the tent with the door open. This weather takes my appetite most all away. Most of the Reg't. went out on picket yesterday for two days but I did not have to go.[3]

Tuesday Feb 2nd [1864]

This morning is very fine. The sun shines very bright and it seems like a day in May at my home. Our Regt. have a good many sick just now. There are about one hundred and thirty excused by the doctor

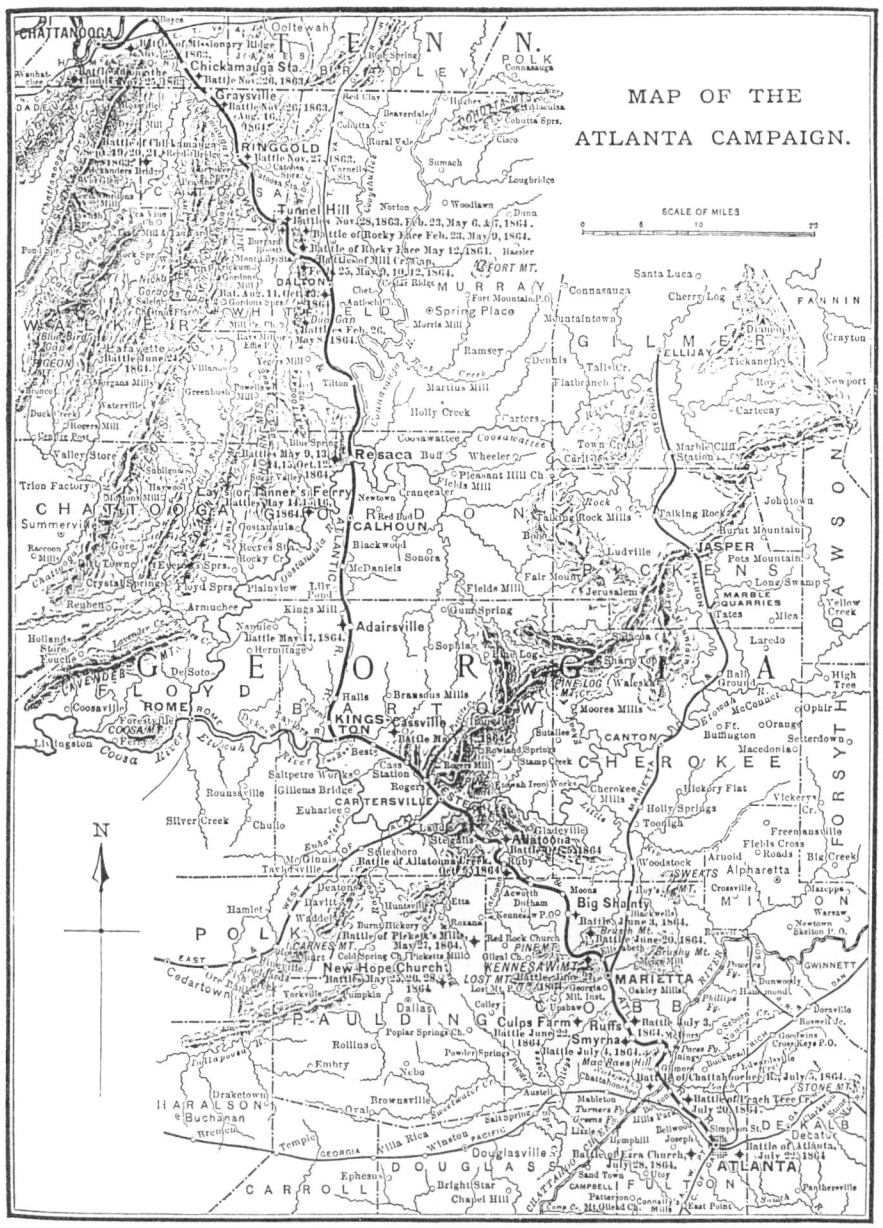

ATLANTA CAMPAIGN 1864
Battles and Leaders of the Civil War, 1886

from duty. There are a great many dead horses and mules that lie unburied about this place and when the hot weather comes I think it will be very unhealthy to live here.

The cars run regular here every day with supplies. It is reported that the enemy have left from our front and where their main force are is not known.

Wednesday [February] 3rd [1864]

The weather has changed some and is colder. It seemed good now to have your coat on. Most of the boys were on picket today. They went out for two days but it was not my turn so I am in camp sitting near a good fire in the fire place.[4]

Monday [February] 15th [1864]

Today we received two months pay. I got $34.[5]

Wed. [February] 17th [1864]

I sent a letter home by Dan True with $37 in it.[6]

Monday [February] 22nd [1864]

Today I have nothing to do. The weather is quite mild again. It has been cold for some time back.[7]

March 22nd, Tuesday [1864]

This morning there is four inches of snow and the snow is still coming very fast.[8]

Wednesday [March] 30th [1864]

Today I went on picket for two days. The picket line is out about 6 miles from our camp, so it is a pretty good walk there. The first day and night was quite cold but the second day was warm and at night it rained some. The guard duty that we have had to do this winter has been easier than it was last, both as concerns the weather and the number of times we have been called to go on picket. The scouts came in and reported they could find no Rebels within 15 miles.[9]

April 10th, Sunday [1864]

Devillo A. Dodge of this company died this morning. He had the measles and then diphtheria set in. He died without a hope of eternal life.[10]

[April] 11th, Monday [1864]

Today we buried Dodge in the Chattanooga Cemetery. We followed him to the grave with military honors. First the corpse then a Corporal with eight men with their guns, then those of the Company that chose to go without arms. The only thing we lacked was a drum and fife. These we did not have in the Regt. Our drum corps is home on a furlough. We fired a salute three times of nine guns each.[11]

[April] 15th, Friday [1864]

Yesterday the Corps was reviewed by Major General Thomas. I was on guard but did not see him. Today I studied an example [math problem] for some time without getting it but after a while I got it.

[April] 17th, Sunday [1864]

This afternoon there was preaching by one of the U.S.C.C. [United States Christian Commission]. His text was "Come unto me all ye that are weary and heavy laden and I will give you rest." He explained what the rest was, and what was required of us in order to obtain this rest.[12]

[April] 30th, Saturday [1864]

Today we were mustered for two months pay.[13]

May 1st, Sunday [1864]

Today we have received orders to march at 5 A.M. tomorrow, Monday.[14]

[May] 2nd, Monday [1864]

We were awake at 3 A.M. to get ready for the march. I was on guard and had to get up at half past twelve and be up till morning, so I had but little sleep. We did not get off until about 7 A.M. and we went about 13 miles where we are camped for the night.

We are east of Chattanooga. It is said that we are within 2 miles of the rebels. I was mistaken in saying we were east of C. We are south of southeast.

[May] 3rd, Tuesday [1864]

Today we have changed our campground and got up tents pretty good but now just at night we have orders to march early in the morning. We have 3 days rations issued tonight and with [the] one that we have already makes four to carry.

[May] 4th, Wednesday [1864]

This morning we were on our way a little after six and marched until one P.M. I should have said that the name of this place that we started from this morning was Gordon's Mills and all the place could show for a building was the mill.

The country is very thinly settled. We are in what is called Pleasant Valley. I have got along so far with the march and feel first rate. Came about 10 miles today. We are very close to the enemy.

[May] 5th, Thursday [1864]

We have not moved today. This is my birthday and I have no cake to eat.

[May] 6th, Friday [1864]

Today we have marched about 7 miles. We went through Nick-a-Jack Gap and are camped on what is called Leach's farm. Every thing looks as though we should have a battle soon.

[May] 7th, Saturday [1864]

This morning we marched at five and camped in Dogwood Valley. The day was very hot. We were ordered to be ready at any time tonight to fall in for a fight. We came 16 miles.

[May] 8th, Sunday [1864]

At noon we were ordered to leave our knapsacks and get ready to march in light order. We advanced about 2 miles when we loaded our guns and sent men to the right and left to protect the flanks. I am with ten men of the Company out about ¼ of a mile to the left of the road. There is some firing in the front.

At 8 P.M. we were called in by the Adjutant and sent back to where we camped last night, which is about four miles. The reason we came back was that the reg't. had orders to go back, so they sent for us to go too but before the reg't. got started, they had orders to stay but these orders came too late for us as we had got into camp before hearing of them. Our reg't. did not get into the fight to day.

[May] 9th, Monday [1864]

This morning we went to the reg't. and took our knapsacks and the teams brought up the mens' to them. We were relieved by the 14th corps today and went back about 5 miles, where we stayed over night. We have not fired a shot yet.

[May] 10th, Tuesday [1864]

It has rained some. We changed our camp to better ground. We have heard no firing to day. It is reckoned that the enemy have left their position and fallen back. The rebels hold what is called Buzzard's Roost, which is a mountain. I am on camp guard today.

[May] 11th, Wednesday [1864]

It rained very hard last night and where we had our tent the water was about two inches deep, so we had to sit up on our knapsacks. I got only about two hours sleep. The bugles blowed at about 2:30 A.M. and we had to get ready to march. The rain had stopped so we made fires & dried our blankets. At day break we were on the road and marched till about one [P.M.] when we camped in Snake [Creek] Gap.

The Gap is 5 miles long and we are in the middle. The enemy are just the other side of the Gap. We came about 12 miles.

[May] 12th, Thursday [1864]

This morning at 10 we moved to the other side of the Gap, 3 miles. Gens. [William T.] Sherman [C.O., U.S. Army in the west], Hooker, Thomas, [John McCauley] Palmer, [John A.] Logan, [James B.] McPherson, [Daniel] Butterfield, and a host of petty generals are all here. There is going to be a grand movement somewhere in these parts.[15]

[May] 13th, Friday [1864]

This morning we marched towards the front 3 miles, where we rested until 11 A.M. when we went to the front and formed a line of battle. Our reg't. is in the 2nd line. There has been some very hard fighting. We were not in it.

[May] 14th, Saturday [1864]

All the afternoon there has been very heavy firing on the left of our line of battle. Tonight I went on the skirmish line from 7 P.M. to 1 A.M. We did not fire nor were we fired on until relieved, when the enemy fired a few shots at us but did not hit any one.[16]

[May] 15th, Sunday [1864]

This has been the hardest fight that the reg't. was ever in. In about 3 hours we lost in our Company 2 killed and 12 wounded and the reg't. lost in all 91 men, as near as I can learn.[17]

At daylight this morning we were moved about 5 miles to the left, where we remained until noon, when we went about 2 miles further and formed a line of battle. This was about 2 P.M. Our line ran along at the foot of a hill. We were the second line of battle. Now began the hard fight.

We charged up the first hill, the balls flying over our heads. Then we went down the hill & up another. When the rebels left their breastwork we followed them. All the while there was a perfect hail of bullets. We drove the rebels off the third hill, when we were ordered to halt.

Thus we drove them off three hills and the last two had breastworks thrown up. The hill that we stopped on had no protection except the breastworks which were poorer than those on the second hill.

By the time we were on the last hill, the regt. ahead of us were so cut up that they fell into our reg't. thus making but one line of battle. The enemy had a cross fire on us. They were mad because we got the last hill and [they were] determined to take it again. For this purpose they charged on the hill three times and every time went back with their ranks all cut up. We would load and fire as often as we could get sight of them but we were too much for them and at last they gave it up.

We were relieved at 6 P.M. by some new troops. After being relieved we went two miles to the rear where we camped for the night. During the night there was some fighting from where we were in the afternoon.[18]

[May] 16th, Monday [1864]

This morning we buried our dead. In our company were 3 to bury. One that we thought was wounded was killed and the other one died of his wounds. We have had 3 killed and 10 wounded. The two that were missing have been found, one was wounded and the other not.

At 10 A.M. we were in pursuit of the rebels and went 12 miles to Fields Mill where we crossed the river and camped for the night.[19]

[May] 17th, Tuesday [1864]

This afternoon we marched 10 miles and camped.[20]

[May] 18th, Wednesday [1864]

This morning we were on the road by daylight and came up to the rear guard of the enemy at 3 P.M. We drove them half a mile when we came to where they had quite a hard place to take when we stopped.

Our reg't. was the advance but at night was relieved from the front by another. We had one man wounded. [The wounded man's name did not get recorded.]

[May] 19th, Thurs. [1864]

Last night the rebels left their breastworks and this morning we started in pursuit. At about noon we came upon them before we knew it. We fell back hoping they would attack us but after waiting two hours we attacked them and drove them two miles, when the darkness stopped the pursuit. The reg't. lost 4 wounded.[21]

[May] 21st, Saturday [1864]

Today we are resting and washing.

[May] 22nd [Sunday, 1864]

Today we moved our camp onto better land. We began to feel like ourselves again, after a rest and wash. Our reg't. could not have stood it to march much longer without rest.

[May] 23rd [Monday, 1864]

This morning we were marching at daylight and went 12 miles. We crossed the [Oostanaula] river and camped near it in line of battle.

[May] 24th, Tuesday [1864]

Today we were again tight onto the heels of the enemy and marched 15 miles. We crossed Sandy Hill near Rogersville only higher and more steep.

[May] 25th, Wednesday [1864]

This morning we marched at 8 A.M. At 2 P.M. we came to our 2nd Division that were fighting. We were soon in the fight. Our reg't. was in the 2nd line of battle. The fighting was very hard and continued until dark. Our loss in the Company was 2 wounded. All of those that were in the first line lost very heavily. The enemy had breastworks and we had none. The fighting was in the woods.

We were relieved at 12 P.M. by the 4th Corps. Thus far the 20th Corps has been the only one to do any thing here. The 14th & 23rd are on the road here.[22]

[May] 26th, Thursday [1864]

Today we have not stirred from our place. There has been some firing on the right and left but little in the center. The 4th, 14th, 20th and 23rd Corps are all here ready to begin the attack at any time and on the right Gen. McPherson, with the 15th, 16th and 17th Corps is expected to do his part of the fighting. We are near to Dallas.

[May] 27th, Friday [1864]

Today there has been some firing but our reg't. is lying back.

[May] 28th, Saturday [1864]

This morning our Company went out on the skirmish line at 5 A.M. and stayed until 6 P.M. While we were out there we had to stay in one place all of the time, without being able to cook any. But when we came out we cooked our suppers. There has been very bad firing on our left this afternoon. We are on the right center of the line.[23]

[May] 29th, Sunday [1864]

There has been no very hard fighting today but tonight about 10 P.M. there was very hard fighting on both the right and left of the line. Our reg't. was lying in the rifle pits but we were not attacked.

We thought that the rebels would charge on the works but they did not. I think by the cheering that I heard on our side that the enemy got the worst of it. I had a bullet go through my bayonet scabbard today. It went through a piece of tent I had in my hands, then struck on a bush and then wounded one of our boys in the leg just below the knee. He was cooking supper at the time.[24]

CAPTAIN ALVIN T. COLE
COMPANY A,
136TH NEW YORK

(Division of Military and Naval Affairs, NYS Adjt. Gen. Office, Albany, NY, Photograph Division, USAMHI)

LEFT: 1ST LIEUTENANT
ALBERT T. SAMPSON,
104TH NEW YORK

RIGHT: 1ST LIEUTENANT EDWARD SILL,
COMPANY K,
136TH NEW YORK

This picture was taken after February 1865, following Sill's second escape from the Confederates.

(Division of Military and Naval Affairs, NYS Adjt. Gen. Office, Albany, NY, Photograph Division, USAMHI)

[May] 30th, Monday [1864]

Tonight we were relieved from the first line of breastworks and were put into the 2nd line. Here we are not in so much danger and can have more sleep.[25]

[May] 31st, Tuesday [1864]

There has been about the same amount of firing as common. I have been Acting Orderly Sergeant since the 15th of the month.[26]

June 1st, Wednesday [1864]

Today at noon we were moved 5 miles to the left of our line of battle. We were relieved by the 15th Corps.[27]

[June] 2nd, Thursday [1864]

At noon today we were moved, still farther to the left of the line, 4 miles. We are either trying to flank the rebels or else they are trying to flank us. There has been about the same amount of fighting as common for the last two days. Just as we were ready to march today it began to rain very hard and [it] lasted an hour.

[June] 3rd, Friday [1864]

At about 2 P.M. we were again on the road and went about 5 miles further to the left. It is the general belief that the rebels are retreating towards Atlanta and only keeping up a line in our front to protect their rear. They have very strong works here that were built 2 years ago. I suppose we do not attack them on account of them having so strong a position. It has rained quite hard this afternoon.[28]

[June] 5th, Sunday [1864]

We have been lying still these two days. The roads are very muddy. Yesterday it rained all day but today it has cleared off.

[June] 6th, Monday [1864]

This morning we marched at 6 A.M. and did not get into position to camp until dark and then we had to build breastworks. We came 5 miles.

[June] 7th, Tuesday [1864]

Today we are resting. I went to the creek and bathed and washed my clothing. At 5 P.M. inspection.

[June] 8th, Wednesday [1864]

Every thing seems to be quiet. There has been a shower today.

[June] 9th, Thursday [1864]

I got my hat by mail last night but did not get a letter. I cannot send one because I am out of postage stamps. The hat was about what I needed.

[June] 11th, [Saturday, 1864]

We have been under marching orders but have not left yet. The supply train is back for rations and cannot get up on account of the bad roads. This keeps us here I suppose and keeps us on rather short allowances of hard-tack and pork. We have not suffered however but will if they do not come soon.

[June] 12th, Sunday [1864]

Rain! Rain! Rain! for the last 12 days we have had rain every day. You can imagine what the roads are about here and why the army does not move. The rations have come up and very acceptable they are.

[June] 13th, [Monday, 1864]

Today it has not rained. I think it is going to be clear. I got some more hard tack.

[June] 14th, Tuesday [1864]

Today has been dry. It does not take long for the country roads to dry, after a rain.

[June] 15th, Wednesday [1864]

Today we started again in pursuit of the rebels. Our Brigade was in the rear of the first. We did not go more than 5 miles before we came up with the enemy. We drove the rebels about a mile when the First

Brigade came to where they could not go any further on account of the rebel breastworks. It was now about sundown. As soon as the rebels were in their works they began to shell us and kept it up until dark. This was the only time that we were in danger. We were lying in a piece of wood during the shelling and the pieces would strike the trees but fortunately for us we did not get hit. We lay in line of battle all night with our knapsacks on.[29]

[June] 16th, Thursday [1864]

This morning very early we built breastworks and have laid in them all day. Tonight we have relieved the First Brigade. This brings us in the first line of battle. The rebels shelled us some tonight.

[June] 17th, Friday [1864]

This morning the rebels are no where to be seen. At noon we started in pursuit and came up with them in going 4 miles. There has been some hard fighting this afternoon but our Division has not got into it.

[June] 18th, Saturday [1864]

It has rained a good part of the day. We have not moved out of our place.

[June] 19th, Sunday [1864]

This morning the rebels are again on the retreat. We started about 9 A.M. and at 2 P.M. came up with them. It rained from about 10 A.M. until noon, very hard and we all got very wet. We sent skirmishers out ahead and advanced in line of battle.

We drove them 2 miles and then came upon their works when we had to halt. We had 4 men of our reg't. wounded.

One died in a few hours. He was shot through the bowels. The line of battle that was in our rear built breastworks and after dark we went back and the second line was the first.[30]

[June] 20th, Monday [1864]

We had one man of our company wounded on the skirmish line. He was struck in the head.[31]

[June] 21st, Tuesday [1864]

This morning we advanced our line about a mile. We lost in the reg't. 5 wounded. We got a hill, which is of importance to us for we can shell the enemy from it.[32]

[June] 22nd, Wednesday [1864]

Today we took another hill. We lost but one in the Reg't. but the Brigade lost 30 men. After we took this hill we built breastworks on it. At the same time we advanced, other troops advanced on the enemy and we were able to join our point all along the line.

At about 5 P.M. the enemy massed his troops (one corps) against the 2nd Division of our corps and seemed determined to break through but they were driven back with great slaughter, while our loss was very light, as we had breastworks behind which to fight. The fight did not get up to us but we could hear it very well. Thus they get the worst of it every time and daily lose ground.

At dark we were relieved by a part of the 4th corps and went about 3 miles to the right. It was ten by the time we got fixed for the night. We are now where we can build fires and get our suppers. Just before the attack began, I started to get my supper but that put a stop to it. I had nothing to eat from early in the morning.[33]

[June] 24th, Friday [1864]

This morning we moved again to the right. We are in the 2nd line of battle. The first is so near that they can talk with the enemy. Our boys will say to the rebs "Look out Johnny here is something to kill you," and they will jeer. The rebs will say, "Look out, Yanks," and then fire. They keep this up for a while and then agree not to fire for some time and go to talking about the war.[34]

[June] 25th, Saturday [1864]

One year ago today we crossed the Potomac on our way to Gettysburg. There has been about the same amount of firing today as common.

[June] 26th, Sunday [1864]

Everything is quiet today.

[June] 27th, Monday [1864]

This morning before light we were relieved and sent back about half a mile. There has been some very hard fighting today. It commenced by our folk opening with artillery.[35]

[June] 28th, Tuesday [1864]

Today everything is quiet again.[36]

[June] 29th, Wednesday [1864]

Tonight we are again in the front line. Everything seems to be quiet with only a shot now and then between pickets.

[June] 30th, Thursday [1864]

Today we are mustered for two months pay but I cannot tell when we shall get it.[37]

July 1st Thursday [1864]

Tonight our folk fired a few shot but did not get any answer. The cannonading was kept up for about half an hour.[38]

[July] 2nd Saturday [1864]

This morning there was a heavy artillery fire opened on the enemy—and some musketry. The rest of the day was quiet.

[July] 3d, Sunday [1864]

This morning the enemy are nowhere to be found. They have fallen back all along the line. We followed them up and did not get to camp until dark.

[July] 4th Monday [1864]

We have stayed in the same place in which we stopped last night until 4 P.M. when we got orders to march, went about 2 miles and camped for the night. We built breastworks but did not use them.

[July] 5th, Tuesday [1864]

This morning we are again on the road. We went to within 2 miles of the river and camped for the night. The rebels left the strongest works

I ever saw. If they cannot hold such ground they cannot hold any.[39]

[July] 6th Wednesday [1864]

At noon today we marched still nearer [to] the Chattahoochee River and at 5 P.M. we halted in the woods and were told that we were to stay here for a few days for rest.

[July] 7th Thurs. [1864]

We are resting and getting clean.

[July] 10th Sunday [1864]

This morning the enemy are all across the river and our pickets are on this bank and the rebel pickets on the other. We are still in the same camp.[40]

[July] 12th, Tues. [1864]

Yesterday the pickets were quite friendly & were trading coffee for tobacco. The weather is very hot. Everything is quiet and we do not hear any firing near.[41]

[July] 17th, Sunday [1864]

This morning at 9, we were told to be ready to march after dinner. At 4 P.M. we started and marched about 5 miles to the railroad which we crossed and then crossed the Chattahoochie River and camped about 2 miles from it. It was 11 P.M. when we stopped.

[July] 18th, Monday [1864]

At about 9 A.M. we were again on the road. We marched in line of battle through the woods most all day and stopped at dark. We did not come across any rebels. I think we came about 8 miles. We must be trying to get into the rear of Atlanta.[42]

[July] 19th, Tuesday [1864]

Our Division has been in the same place all day. We were told in the morning to be ready to march at a moment's notice but at night were told that we would stay here for the night. We were told that an

Official Dispatch has been received that Gen. McPherson and Branseau had cut the railroad in the rear of Atlanta. That will make the reb dig out if anything will.

[July] 20th, Wed. [1864]

This morning we were up and had our breakfast at daylight but did not get started until 8 o'clock. We went about 3 miles when we came up with the enemy.

Our reg't. sent out 3 companies as skirmishers and were soon engaged with the enemy. The rebels came out of their works and met us like men and at first our men gave way but it was not long before we drove them off the battle ground and we held it with all their dead and wounded and a great many prisoners. We captured a rebel flag but the man [Private Dennis Buckley, Co. G] was killed who got it.[43]

[July] 21st Thurs. [1864]

This morning the battle field is in our possession and men are at work carrying off the wounded and burying the dead. Our company is on the skirmish line today. We fire some but we are so far off that the bullets will hardly reach.[44]

[July] 22nd, Friday [1864]

This morning the enemy are gone and we are on the move. We came up with them when we were about 2½ miles from Atlanta, where we stopped and built breastworks. We are near enough to shell the town.

[July] 23d Saturday [1864]

Today we moved to the right of our corps and are on the railroad 2 miles from the city. Tonight our artillery have fired and shot every five minutes into the city of Atlanta. The enemy replied but feebly. We moved our line still nearer to the enemy during the night and put up strong earthworks.

[July] 25th Monday [1864]

Our skirmishers have kept up a steady fire today and the artillery have done their part. The enemy have a very strong position here and it would seem, plenty of artillery. Tonight we have been relieved from the front line and have gone into the second. When we were in the first line one fourth of the reg't. had to sit up, to watch, all night long and in the second line we only have a guard.[45]

[July] 26th Tuesday [1864]

Today one of the reg't. of the Corps made an attack on the enemy's picket line, just after our artillery had been firing very fast and captured over 30 of the enemy.[46]

[July] 28th Thurs. [1864]

There has been a very bad fight on the right of the line about 4 miles from the railroad. The rebels charged our works 3 times and were driven back with heavy loss. The whole battlefield is in our possession. We started to go to the help of our men but before we got far, news came that we were not needed.[47]

[July] 29th Friday [1864]

Today we were moved to the right of the line and have put up breastworks beyond the battlefield. It was very hot today and the sun made most every one sick. I never had the sun affect me at home as it does down here.

[July] 30th Saturday [1864]

We advanced our line some without meeting any large force of the enemy.

[July] 31st Sunday [1864]

It is very hot today. Some troops are moving but we have only been out a mile and came back into camp. It was said we went for a support to some other troops. There was a nice shower tonight, making the air cooler.[48]

Aug. 1st [Monday 1864]

Everything quiet.

[August] 2nd [Tuesday 1864]

We are making out the pay rolls for the last 2 months. We expect to get six months pay soon. At 4 o'clock we got orders to march, [and we] went back the same road [by which] we came here and camped just at dark in a piece of woods.[49]

[August] 3d Wednesday [1864]

This morning we took our place on the line, near where we were before we went to the right of the line. Tonight most of the men are out building works nearer to the enemy.[50]

[August] 4th Thurs. [1864]

Today we took the front line and relieved a brigade of the 14th Corps. They are still working on the works in front of us and by tomorrow they will be ready for us to reoccupy.

[August] 5th Friday [1864]

We went tonight into the new works in our front. We are getting pretty near Atlanta. Our picket line is within ¾ of a mile of the City. They keep up a pretty steady fire and it is dangerous for a Johnny to show his head.

We are in a piece of woods, so it is quite pleasant. Tomorrow we are to get a day and a half rations of soft bread, the first we have had since May 1st.[51]

[August] 6th [Saturday 1864]

We have got our tents up and think we shall stay here for a few days.[52]

[August] 7th Sunday [1864]

Everything is quiet. We are to have inspection at 5 P.M. We have roll call night and morning.

[August] 8th Monday [1864]

This morning we advanced our line on to the next hill in front. The breastworks were built last night.

[August] 9th [Tuesday 1864]

Today we were relieved from the front line and took the second line in the same place we left yesterday.

[August] 10th Wed. [1864]

A part of the men are building works on the hill in front of the front lines, then there will only be a short valley between our line and the line of the rebels.[53]

[August] 13th Saturday [1864]

We moved today into the front line of works that the men have been building. We are in plain sight of the rebels' works.[54]

[August] 20th Saturday [1864]

For the past week we have stayed in the same place and nothing for us to do. Some balls passed over our works but all we have wounded is one.

One bullet went through my tent the other day but did no more damage than to make a hole for the rain to come through.[55]

[August] 21st Sunday [1864]

Today it has rained some. All is quiet.

[August] 25th, Thurs. [1864]

Up to last night every thing remained the same but last night, a part of the troops left us. I do not know where they went. Rumor says that we shall probably go tonight.

[August] 26th Friday [1864]

Last night we left our breastworks and went back 7 miles to the Chattahoochie River. We got back at daybreak and here we found a part of the Corps that went back the night before. They had breastworks put up for us to go into and we are told we are sent here to guard this which is called Turner's Ferry. Our Brigade and one other is here.[56]

[August] 27th, Saturday [1864]

Today the enemy attacked us but were driven off without loss to us. One reb was wounded.

[August] 28th Sunday [1864]

Today we are making our works stronger.[57]

[August] 29th [Monday 1864]

I am writing most of today. We will be mustered for 2 months more pay, on the 31st.[58]

[August] 30th Tues. [1864]

Today we had two men taken [prisoner] and one killed by the rebels. They were outside the picket line without their arms. They went out to get some milk.[59]

[5 pages missing from the original document.]

Commentary:
On September 4, the regiment with its brigade (3rd BG, 3rd Div., XX) moved into Atlanta and settled down for the occupation of the city. During that time, its recruiting detachment back in New York set off for the front with 67 recruits, 11 of whom deserted before leaving the state. The remaining six losses for the month were almost evenly distributed between death from disease, death from wounds, and discharge from the service. The regiment entered the following month with 277 effectives and an additional 252 absent from duty.[60]

Nothing of real importance happened in October, either. The regiment lost eight men during the month to various causes. (Refer to Appendix D).

Oct. 9th Sunday [1864]

This morning I attended church in Atlanta for the first time. There were 3 of the U.S.C.C. [United States Christian Commission] that held the service and one of them preached a very good sermon. After meeting I went and took dinner with Lieut. True and a good one too. Last night was cold and today cold even with sunshine.

Nov. 5th Saturday [1864]

Today at noon orders came to march. At 3 P.M. we started & went about 3 miles south of the city and camped for the night.

[November] 8th, Sunday [1864]

It is clearing up this morning. Just after dinner time we were ordered back into camp where we were very much to go into our old tents.

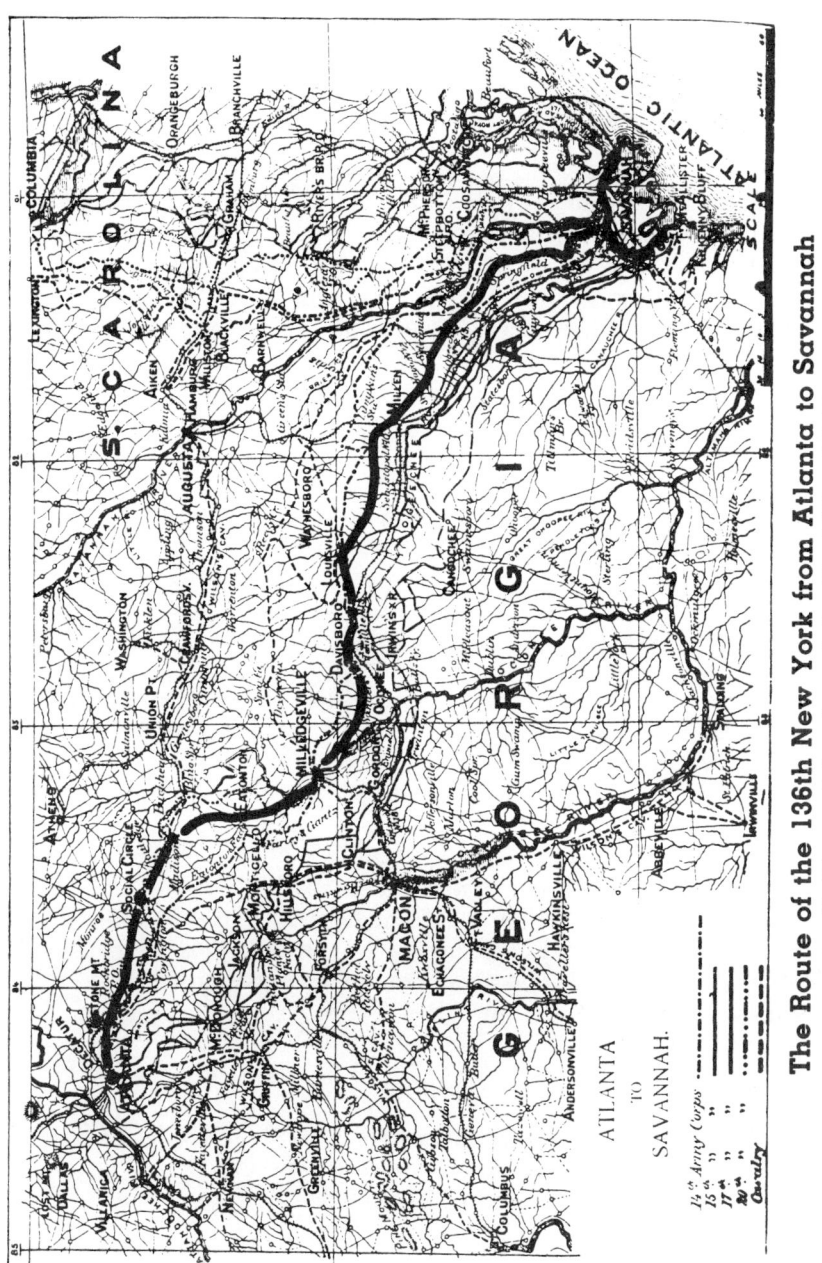

The Route of the 136th New York from Atlanta to Savannah
Battles and Leaders of the Civil War, 1886

It rained some this afternoon. A few rebels made their appearance and fired on our picket line. They killed one, and captured one, but he escaped.

[November] 9th, Wed. [1864]

This morning, just after roll call, the rebels attacked us on the left, and in about one hour they attacked us on the right. There is about 2 miles between the two places. They did not appear in front of our reg't. We were ordered to pack everything except our tents.

It is now afternoon and everything is quiet, no firing on the line. We expect a campaign to begin very soon. We are ordered to draw all the clothing we shall want for the next fifty days.[61]

[November] 12th, Saturday [1864]

We are still in Atlanta. All is quiet. Yesterday we were drilled twice which does not seem like leaving very soon. Sometimes it seems as if we would start off immediately then again as if we were to stay our time out in Atlanta. The weather is cool and pleasant.

[November] 14th Monday [1864]

Orders have come to be ready to march in the morning and we have each 4 days rations of bread, 5 of sugar, 10 of coffee and salt, and 2 days of meat.

[November] 15th, Tues. [1864]

This morning at 9 A.M. we were on the road to Augusta and marched rather slowly until 3 P.M. when we stopped to get our dinner and then marched until the next morning at 7 A.M. when we stopped to rest and get breakfast. The reason of our being on the road all night was that we were in the rear of the Corps. We marched 16 miles.

[November] 16th, Wednesday [1864]

At 11 A.M. we marched and camped about 9 P.M. a distance of 18 miles. We are getting into a country where forage is plenty, such as sweet potatoes, corn, cattle, hogs and some sheep.

[November] 17th, Thurs. [1864]

Started at 5 A.M. and went into camp at 8 P.M. I got all the sweet potatoes I wished to eat. Saw some very good looking women but not a man in sight unless cripples or very old. Marched 20 miles.[62]

[November] 18th Friday [1864]

Marched at 6 A.M. and went 5 miles to a town named Social Circle, of 2000 inhabitants. Here we tore up the railroad and burned it & went on 11 miles more and camped at midnight.[63]

Saturday [November] 19th [1864]

Today we came to Madison, the best looking place I have ever seen in the South. We burned the railroad and all public buildings and also the house they used for whipping slaves in. The negroes are flocking to us by the hundreds. Camped at 3 P.M. just outside the town. Started at 5 A.M. & came 15 miles.[64]

Sunday [November] 20th [1864]

Started at 6 A.M. and camped at 4 P.M. It rained a little this morning. Feet quite sore. Marched 15 miles.

Monday [November] 21st [1864]

This morning it rains quite hard. Marched at day light and were train guard. We passed through Eaton and camped before dark. It has stopped raining. Went 14 miles.

Tuesday [November] 22nd [1864]

We are within 12 miles of the capital of the State. [We] marched at 8 A.M. and camped in Milledgeville at 3 P.M. It is quite cold tonight.

Wednesday [November] 23rd [1864]

We do not march. I had my clothes [washed] today. The capital is a very good size place and the streets are all very regularly laid out. All of the public buildings are being destroyed today.

Gov. Bratton left for parts unknown when he heard that we were coming. All but the darkies are gone and most of these will go with us. It is just one year since I went into the battle of Chattanooga.

Thursday [November] 24th [1864]

This morning at 7 A.M. we marched out of the town and crossed a small river. (Its name I do not know. [Oconee River]). Here we stopped until after dinner when we marched until the next morning at 5 A.M. only stopping for our supper.

The night was quite cold and we had the fences burning to keep warm by. We only went 10 miles.

Friday [November] 25th [1864]

Today our whole reg't. went out for forage. I got lots of sweet potatoes, two chickens and some bacon.

[We] went 14 miles. The army [went] only ten and camped at 8 P.M. The country is full of small swamps.

Saturday [November] 26th [1864]

Started at 7 A.M. and went through one swamp 2 miles long. I had boiled chicken for breakfast. Camped at 3 P.M. at Sandersville. Marched 10 miles. 2,000 [miles] for [the] yr.

Sunday [November] 27th [1864]

Started at 11 A.M. and marched until 1 P.M., when we camped at Davidsberg. This is a place of about 10 houses on the Georgia Central Railroad.

An old negro in Sandersville said as we went by "My brethren, I have been waiting a long time for you to come and, praise de Lord, you have come. I pray de Lord, my brethren, for you. Dat you might come to us. Now, my brethren, do not laugh at me. I mean all dat I say."

This strange speech made the boys laugh and those that say they are not fighting for the negro hung their heads and could say nothing. At any rate the darky believed that God sent us to deliver them out of their bondage. We were marching quite fast when I heard this speech so I could only hear a little of it. He rubbed his hands all the while as though it was cold weather. Went 13 miles.

[November] 28th Monday [1864]

Marched at 7 A.M. and went 10 miles and camped at noon near the Ogeechee River.

[November] 29th Tuesday [1864]

We were ordered to be ready at 8 A.M. but did not start until 11 and crossed the river. I had a good sleep last night to make up for [the] last time. We went 4 miles and camped, when we were ordered to go one mile further to guard a bridge. Got into camp just after dark.

[November] 30th [Wednesday 1864]

As we do not march today I had my clothing washed. Negroes are flocking to us. Some whole families are coming with us. Some women have 3 and 4 little ones from 6 months old up. I have seen a mother carrying one and one walking in front of her and one behind her hanging on for dear life and besides she would carry a bundle on her head, all of them barefooted.[65]

Dec 1st Thursday [1864]

At 2 P.M. started, went 10 miles and camped at midnight.

[December] 2nd Friday [1864]

Started at 9 A.M.; went 14 miles; camped, 8 P.M.

[December] 3rd [Saturday 1864]

Started at 6 A.M.

Conclusion:

By December 21, William Tecumseh Sherman's army was in Savannah, Georgia. In January 1865, the army moved north into South Carolina and North Carolina where it took part in actions at Fayetteville, Averasboro, Bentonville, Raleigh and Bennett House.

The regiment split up on June 12 with 48 of the men transferring into the 60th New York to finish out their terms of enlistment. On June 13, the remaining number of men who were still in the field with the regiment—around 368 officers and men mustered out of Federal service. The remaining 123 soldiers, who were scattered all over the East from New York City to Louisville, Kentucky were gradually accounted for and/or hunted out to be sworn out of Federal service. The last man mustered out was Morris H. Coats (Co. A), who was in a hospital in Elmira, New York.

John McMahon, who finished the war as the 1st sergeant of Company E, left behind a unique glimpse into the life of the average enlisted man. He was as unflappable and as unmoved as the men with whom he served. He recorded what he saw and what he thought was important and nothing more—much like a person would today who might keep a diary about his/her daily routine. He captured the little things which the historian, in search of the "bigger picture," often overlooks but which the person who experienced the event could not.

Commentary:

The 136th New York was not a "fighting regiment" in the sense of the 69th New York or the 14th Brooklyn and yet it served just as steadfastly as the best of the Northern regiments. Throughout its service, the regiment suffered from the same problems as any regiment on both sides. Casualties, while not extraordinary, provide a glimpse of the hardships faced by the 19th Century infantryman. The losses of the 136th New York represent a cross section of the ills which typically befell a regiment. It is interesting to note how many men "died" without noting the cause and how many expired from unnamed diseases.

During its 30 months of active duty the regiment had 162 men (27% of the losses) discharged for disabilities with most of them (92) occurring during the first hard campaigning of 1863. That same year 40 men resigned or received discharges. By the end of the war discharges accounted for 89 losses (14%). Desertion claimed 11% of the casualties (69) with most of them occurring in 1863. Combat related injuries and/or illnesses sent 63 men (10% of the losses) into the Veteran Reserve Corps. Disease (52 men—8%), absent and unaccounted for (44 soldiers—7%), and killed in action (41 men—6%) claimed the bulk of the remaining casualties. Despite its relatively light casualties the regiment lost 20 people per month. Those who had become partially disabled but not totally incapacitated often ended up in the Veteran Reserve Corps, which the men called the "Invalid Corps." Scattered to different barracks throughout the Union, the Veteran Reserve battalions were supposed to defend strategic areas within the Union against Confederate attack. In July 1864, the Veteran Reserve Corps temporarily held Fort Stevens in Washington, DC, until the VI Corps arrived to repel Jubal Early's attack on the Capital.

1863 was the shakedown year with the depletion rate decreasing with each succeeding year. As the soldiers became more toughened from harder marching and more exposure to the elements, the weak sloughed off rapidly and the survivors immune system acclimated to army life. Their calloused attitudes translated into a "hard nosed" no nonsense business oriented United States after the war.

FOOTNOTES

1. Discharged with a disability: January 5 — 1st Lt. Isaac Johnson (Co. D).
   Transferred to the VRC: January 9 — Cpl. Edwin Bliss (Co. A).

2. Resigned: January 11 — 1st Lt. Anson Hall (Co. H) "for the good of the service."
   Died from disease: January 16 — William Altoft (Co. D).
   Discharged: January 16 — Avery Eager (Co. D).
   Discharged for disability: Cpl. John McCray (Co. H), who was paralyzed.
   Died from disease: January 19 — Cpl. Pliny L. Metcalf (Co. D) from chronic diarrhea.
   Discharged with a disability: Cpl. Elias Hoyt (Co. D).

3. Discharged with a disability: John Hammond (Co. C).
   The 136th New York was at its highest enrollment since the beginning of the war. 799 officers and men were on the rolls of whom 542 reported for duty with the regiment. The absentees include 133 officers and men were on detached service with the division.
   TAGO, Record Group 94, Muster Rolls, Returns, Regimental Papers, Box 3294, Volunteer Organizations of the Civil War, New York, 136th Inf., Return for January 1864.

4. Died of disease: Cpl. Henry C. Wing (Co. D) died while he was on furlough.
   Died: February 11 — Edward Keel (Co. D) while a prisoner of war in Richmond, Virginia.
   Discharged with a disability: February 14 — Sgt. Charles Beedle (Co. I).

5. Died of disease: Henry Neff (Co. G) from lung inflammation.

6. Discharged with a disability: John Gill (Co. I).
   Died from disease: February 18 — Henry C. Jones (Co. G) from chronic diarrhea.
   Died: February 18 — Oliver Dean (Co. I).

7. Disease and discharges accounted for the remaining five losses to the 136th New York for the balance of that month.
   Died of disease: February 23 — Derious German (Co. K) from fever.
   Died: February 23 — James M. Slate (Co. F).
   Resigned: February 24 — Cpt. James Cameron (Co. D), upon the orders of Major General Thomas for "shiftlessness and incompetency."
   Died: February 27 — David C. Wade (Co. I) while on furlough.
   Discharged: February 28 — John Williams (Co. F).
   TAGO, Record Group 94, Descriptive Rolls, Field and Staff, Volunteer Organizations of the Civil War, New York, 136th Inf., 6.
   On the positive side 11 new recruits were picked up in New York, which reduced the regiment's losses to only 1 for that month. Enrollment stood at 763 men, 498 of whom could be counted as effectives. Only 1 officer and 1 enlisted man were AWOL. March came in like the traditional "lion."
   By the time McMahon made his next entry, thirteen men had either died, been transferred to the Veteran Reserve Corps, or had been discharged. (See Appendix B). The two most noteworthy men were Harlow Dudley and William Grant, both in Company H. Dudley died from lung inflammation due to the

hard weather and small pox killed Grant, who was the only victim to that dreaded illness in the regiment.

Office of the Adjutant General, Record Group 94, Muster Rolls, Returns, Regimental Papers, Box 3294, Volunteer Organizations of the Civil War, New York, 136th Inf., Return for February 1864.

8. Transferred: Cpl. Chester Warriner (Co. H) into the U.S. Signal Corps.
   Died: Cpl. Whipple Davis (Co. I) in Springwater, New York.
   Died: March 29 — Sgt. Jacob Dieter (Co. I) at Belle Island, Richmond, Virginia, as a prisoner of war.

   In the meantime the recruiters in New York picked up an additional two recruits.

9. Regimental strength dropped to 623 of which 61% (383 officers and men) could be counted as effectives. The sick rolls had finally dropped to below 100 men by the end of this month.

   TAGO, Record Group 94, Muster Rolls, Returns, Regimental Papers, Box 3294, Volunteer Organizations of the Civil War, New York, 136th Inf., Return for March 1864.

10. Discharged with disability: April 5 — John Heller (Co. B).
    Transferred into the VRC: April 10 — George Woolhiser (Co. K).

11. Died of Disease: Cpl. Edward Kellogg (Co. D) in the hospital.
    Died: April 12 — Sgt. Homer Emery (Co. D).
    Discharged with disability: April 13 — Peter Mus (Co. H).

12. Died of disease: Isaac T. Williams (Co. G) from chronic diarrhea.
    Transferred to the VCR: April 22 — George H. White (Co. A).
    Discharged with disability: April 27 — James B. Paul (Co. H).

13. The regiment stood at 423 effectives of a total enrollment of 590. The sick list was down to 69 enlisted men and 1 officer.

    TAGO, Record Group 94, Muster Rolls, Returns, Regimental Papers, Box 3294, Volunteer Organizations of the Civil War, New York, 136th Inf., Return for April 1864.

14. Transferred to the VRC: Russell Mann (Co. H).

15. Discharged with a disability: Samuel A. Wolcott (Co. H).

    McPherson commanded the Army of the Tennessee. Palmer, Logan and Butterfield were corps commanders.

16. McMahon erred in this statement. Cpt. Willard Chapin (Co. C) received a wound during the action.

17. The records show 13 enlisted men killed, 1 officer and 11 enlisted men mortally wounded, 3 officers and 53 enlisted men wounded, and 1 enlisted man missing.
    (Phisterer, IV, 1912, 3582)

18. McMahon's description is much more precise than the one given in the *Official Records*. 13 enlisted men died outright. 1 officer, 1st Lt. William Hall (Co. A), and 11 enlisted men were mortally wounded. 3 officers and 53 men

recovered from their wounds and 1 man was missing for a total of 82 combat related casualties. John Gavagan (Co. B) did not get lost. He deserted. Henry Schrauder (Co. E) died from his wounds on the day he received them. (See Appendix C for casualties.) John G. Rouse (Co. A) went into the Veteran Reserve Corps.

19. Died of wounds: Ammi Perkins (Co. C).
Wounded in action: Joshua Sanford (Co. B) and John Bowen (Co. D).
Killed in action: George T. Worden (Co. H).

20. Died of wounds: Harvey E. Pond (Co. D) and Charles Carroll (Co. E).

21. Wounded in action: Elisha Herdendorf (Co. E) and Samuel R. Yencer (Co. F).

22. Captured in action: 1st Lt. Edward Sill (Co. K).
Wounded in action: George L. Telford (Co. D), who never showed up in the regimental records again and James Jones (Co. G). Company E's losses did not get recorded by name.

At this time, the 136th New York belonged to the Third Brigade, Third Division, XX Corps.

23. Transferred to the VRC: William Ayling and James Lavery, and Frederick Litz (all from Co. E).
Died of wounds: 1st Lt. William Hall (Co. A).
Wounded in action: Edward Lynch (Co. E) while on the skirmish line.

24. Wounded in action: Mathias Eker (Co. H).

25. Died of disease: Alturna C. Smith (Co. H) from cerebritus—brain inflammation as a result of blood poisoning.

26. Transferred to the VRC: John Hendrick and James Kelly (both Co. F).
The regiment now had 566 men on the books. 53% (300 effectives) could report for duty.
TAGO, Record Group 94, Muster Rolls, Returns, Regimental Papers, Box 3294, Volunteer Organizations of the Civil War, New York, 136th Inf., Return for May 1864.

27. Died of wounds: Alexander C. Mathews (Co. K).

28. Wounded in action: Daniel B. Whipple (Co. H).
Killed in action: John Warheight (Co. H).

29. The brigade bivouacked about 100 yards from the Confederate works, which were stretched across the Sandtown Road. During the skirmishing, rounds hit John Lewis (Co. B), Andrew Clute (Co. F) and Newton Neff (Co. G).
Transferred to the VRC: George Kuhn (Co. I).

30. The fighting took place along the Dallas and Marietta Road near Noyes' Creek, Georgia. The brigade deployed to the right of the road and pushed the Confederates back to within 100 yards of the Confederate works. The adjutant recorded three of the four casualties.
Died of wounds: Harrison Clemens (Co. I).
Wounded in action: Ira W. Sherwood (Co. F) and Dominique Kneip (Co. G).
(OR, XXXVIII, Part 2, 439)

31. Wounded in action: James Dow (Co. E).

32. The 136th New York and the 55th Ohio took part in the reconnaissance to the right of the brigade line. The 73rd Ohio reinforced the expedition, which lasted from 11:00 A.M. until 6:00 P.M. when the three regiments occupied the hill mentioned by McMahon. The 136th New York lost six men, one of whom was captured.
    Wounded in action: Cpl. James M. Decker (Co. C), Seeley Foote (Co. H), William Close (Co. I), Cpl. George Coon and James McKee (both from Co. K).
    Captured in action: Edward Milner (Co. H).
    Died of disease: Wallace Griffith (Co. D) in the hospital.

33. Again John McMahon's description is as good as the one in the Official Records.
    Wounded in action: Henry Curtis (Co. E) and Peter Chapman (Co. F).

34. Died of wound: Cpl. Russel P. Wescott (Co. I).

35. Wounded in action: George Snyder (Co. K). — 2nd time

36. Wounded in action: Cpl. William H. Ward (Co. C).
    Died of disease: Jacob Lafosce (Co. B) from chronic diarrhea.

37. Died of wound: Edward Lynch (Co. E).
    Discharged: Jacob Post (Co. F).
        Counting the one recruit picked up during the month, the regiment stood at 550 officers and enlisted personnel. 284 (51%) could report for service. The sick list had climbed to 168 officers and enlisted men. 90 soldiers were on detached duty.
        TAGO, Record Group 94, Muster Rolls, Returns, Regimental Papers, Box 3294, Volunteer Organizations of the Civil War, New York, 136th Inf., Return for June 1864.

38. Died of disease: Cpl. George H. Sanger (Co. C) from fever.

39. The regiment crossed to the western side of Nick-a-Jack Creek and bivouacked two miles from the Chattahoochee River.
    Discharged with disability: 2nd Lt. Robert Bullard (Co. I).
    Died of disease: Benjamin Pond (Co. D).
    Transferred to the VRC: W. Seymore Babcock and James Bacon (both from Co. B).

40. Wounded in action: John Baker (Co. K).
    Died of wounds: John Lewis (Co. B).

41. Wounded in action: Martin Graham (Co. D) by accident.

42. The brigade was deployed by 5:00 P.M. near Buck Head, Georgia to the left of the Buck Head Road and south of the Decatur Road.
    Died of disease: George Gottschall (Co. B) from typhus.
        (OR, XXXVIII, Part 2, 441)

43. The 136th New York covered the brigade's advance at Peach Tree Creek. Deployed to the right of the line between other Federal units, it was to buy

time for the division to deploy. In the ensuing engagement, the skirmishers went into action with other units and not their own brigade.

Dennis Buckley knocked the color bearer of the 31st Mississippi down with his rifle butt. While jubilantly waving the captured flag at the Confederate lines, a bullet glanced off the flagstaff and struck Buckley in the forehead, killing him instantly. His Medal of Honor was given to his mother after the war.

Wounded in action: Hiram Hitchcock and James Mead (both from Co. A), Burr Summers (Co. C), Edward Crowel (Co. D), Cpl. James Fanning (Co. G), who was never heard from again, and Gaskard Keiper (Co. G).

Killed in action: Dennis Buckley and Samuel Whitmore (both from Co. G).

2 men died outright. 1 man died from his wounds. 1 was captured, 1 officer and 13 others were wounded.

(OR, XXXVIII, part 2, 22, 441-444)
(Doty, 1905, 477)

44. Wounded in action: Jacob Stieh (Co. F).

45. Wounded in action: David B. Price (Co. I).

46. Wounded in action: Marcus Knowlton (Co. K).
    Resigned: July 27 — Assistant Surgeon John R. Smith because of a disability and for being absent without leave.
    TAGO, Record Group 94, Descriptive Rolls, Field and Staff, Volunteer Organizations of the Civil War, New York, 136th Inf., 2.

47. Died of wounds: Elisha Herdendorf (Co. E).

48. By the end of July, the regiment, including its three recruits, carried 557 men on the books. 286 men were present for duty.
    TAGO, Record Group 94, Muster Rolls, Returns, Regimental Papers, Box 3294, Volunteer Organizations of the Civil War, New York, 136th Inf., Return for July 1864.

49. Sick in hospital: No further record — John Burns (Co. C).

50. Wounded in action: William W. Stannard (Co. A) by picket fire.

51. Transferred to the VRC: George Drehmer (Co. B).

52. Died of wounds: Cpl. William H. Ward (Co. C).

53. Sick in hospital: No further record — Martin Anderson (Co. B).
    Died of disease: August 11 — Patrick Finn (Co. B) from an abscess.
    Wounded in action: August 12 — 1st Sergeant Theron Cross (Co. K).

54. Wounded in action: August 18 — Robert Green (Co. F).
    August 19 — William Jetty (Co. A).

55. Discharged for disability: Cpt. Edward Pratt (Co. B).

56. Discharged with a disability: Seward Pearson (Co. B).

57. Died of disease: William Flint (Co. D).

58. Died: Alfred Marsh (Co. H).

59. The Confederate guerillas killed James Bradon and captured William Hendrickson (both of Co. K). They also captured Andrew Naughton (Co. D.)
    The Veteran Reserve Corps took Lorenzo Curtis (Co. H) into its ranks on the last day of the month.
    Regimental rolls stood at 537 officers and enlisted personnel. Absent from duty climbed to 287 commissioned and enlisted personnel. Sick roll increased to 191 soldiers. 86 of the regiment's personnel were on detached duty.
    TAGO, Record Group 94, Descriptive Rolls, Field and Staff, Volunteer Organizations of the Civil War, New York, 136th Inf., 121-122.

60. TAGO, Record Group 94, Muster Rolls, Returns, Regimental Papers, Box 3294, Volunteer Organizations of the Civil War, New York, 136th Inf., Return for October 1864.

61. Discharged with a disability: November 11 — Charles Maxon (Co. H).

62. Died of disease: William Ellison (Co. F).
    Discharged for disability: Clarence Lynn (Co. G).
    Captured in action: No further record — Oren Wilson (Co. D).

63. Transferred to the VRC: Ruel Albro (Co. A).
    Transferred from the VRC: Dwight Ferris (Co. A).

64. Transferred to the VRC: George Baker and Hosea Webster (both from Co. D).
    Paroled: Levi Gernsey (Co. H) by the Confederates in Savannah, Georgia.

65. By the end of November, the regiment carried 531 men on the rolls. Effectives numbered 271 men.
    TAGO, Record Group 94, Muster Rolls, Returns, Regimental Papers, Box 3294, Volunteer Organizations of the Civil War, New York, 136th Inf., Return for November 1864.

Postscript

John T. McMahon did not stay in Lima, New York after the war. He married Sarah D. Douglas of Penn Yan, New York in her hometown on August 22, 1870. His father, Isaiah McMahon, presided over the ceremony as the minister. John was 26 years old. Sarah was 20 years old. During their 26 years together, Sarah bore five children and John pursued his religious calling. He and Sarah became missionaries to India and John died there in Dwarahat, N. W. Province on July 5, 1896 at age 52.

Sarah McMahon returned to the United States after John's death and resided at 176 Garfield Place, Brooklyn, New York. In August 1908, she applied for her husband's Civil War pension. In September 1908 Sarah's brother, S. Bainbridge and John's sister, Laura A. McMahon, swore affadivits attesting to Sarah's marriage. Doctor Mary E. Bryan, who in 1896 was the physician for the women's Foreign Missionary Society, verified John's death and where it occurred. On September 24, 1908, ten days after the Pension Office received the affidavits, Sarah McMahon was awarded her pension of $12.00 per month, retroactive to May 19, 1908. Sarah received her husband's pension until her death on February 22, 1915. She was 65 years old and living with her son, J. R. McMahon in Little Falls, New Jersey.

Appendix A

Casualty Returns for the Last Two Days at Gettysburg

Key: DOD—died of disease
DES—deserted
DSGD DIS—discharged with disability
DSGD—discharged
VRC—Veteran Reserve Corps
ABS—absent: no further record
MIA/CIA—missing/captured in action
DOW—died of wounds
KIA—killed in action

July 2, 1863
Company A
Charles Finch—WIA
Martin Finch—WIA
Michael Galvin, Jr.—WIA
Clinton Miner—WIA
Silas R. Pire—WIA
George A. White—WIA
Cpl. Jacob Henry Whiteman—WIA

Company C
Leman B. Withey—WIA

Company E
Patrick Duffy—WIA
Cpl. John Fiero—WIA

Company F
Jeremiah Cullinan—WIA
Elisha Herdendorf—WIA
Joseph Herdendorf—WIA
Henry Limerick—WIA
Gilbert Rulapaugh—WIA

Company H
George Mosher—WIA

Company K
Zack Barber—WIA
Musician Samuel King—WIA

July 3, 1863
Company A
Alonzo Crandall—WIA
William Vanpelt—WIA

Company B
James Bacon—WIA
Aaron Baker—KIA
Cpl. Lucius Bradley—WIA
William Edwards—WIA
Cpl. Dorr Faulkner—WIA
Elias Gage—KIA
Edwin Luce—WIA
William McWhorter—KIA
2nd Lt. Isaac Drake—CIA
Cpl. George Gibbs—KIA

Company C
Thomas Boyle—WIA
James Briggs—WIA
William Du Bois—WIA
Michael Geimer—WIA
Wells Nash—WIA
Monroe Annis—WIA

Company D
Martin Graham—WIA
Cpl. Aaron Walker—WIA

APPENDIX A

July 3, 1863 (cont'd.)
Company E
Nicholas Connor—WIA
James Doren—KIA
James Lavery—WIA
Sgt. James Hanigan—KIA
Lelotas C. Wiggins—KIA

Company F
Cpl. Joseph Malone—WIA
Jacob Post—KIA
Marsena Stout—WIA

Company G
John Folmsbee—WIA
Cpl. John Hayen—WIA
Sgt. William Hover—KIA
Samuel Whitmore—WIA
Isaac T. Williams—CIA

Company H
Charles Elwell—KIA
Cpl. William Noonan—WIA-ABS
Arzy West—KIA
Francis M. Wood—WIA

Company I
Daniel Confer—WIA
Cpl. James Conlon—WIA
Milton Flory—WIA
George Kuhn—WIA

Company K
Peter Connor-WIA
Simeon Ikins—WIA
Sgt. Alonzo Wicks—KIA

During the Battle
Company B
John Wright—WIA
Seward J. Pearson—WIA
John B. Ray—WIA
William K. Selden—WIA
Cpl. Lovett Sherwood—WIA
Richard Youells—WIA

Company G
Cpl. Lucien J. Smith—WIA

Company H
Peter Mus—WIA
John Stowell—WIA

Company I
Samuel Dye

Company K
Cpl. Jerome Isenhour

Appendix B

Losses between March 1 and 22, 1864

1st — Thomas Driscoll (Co. G)—VRC
       Harlow Dudley (Co. H)—DIED—lung inflammation
2nd — John Clark (Co. A)—VRC
       William Du Bois (Co. C)—VRC
3rd — Wells Nash (Co. C)—DSGD DIS
4th — William W. Warner (Co. D)—DSGD
7th — William Grant (Co. H)—DIED—smallpox
       Thomas Boyle (Co. C)—VRC
8th — Samuel Dye (Co. I)—DSGD DIS
15th — Michael Geimer (Co. C)—VRC
       William Hewitt (Co. F)—VRC
       Corporal Jacob Henry Whiteman (Co. A)—VRC
18th — William Mix (Co. D)—DSGD DIS

Appendix C

Casualties from Resaca, Georgia, May 15, 1864.

Company A
Sergeant Aaron Gee—WIA
Samuel Green—WIA
1st Lieutenant William Hall—WIA
Sergeant Alvin White—KIA

Company B
John Gavagan—DES
James Littles—KIA
John Vogt—KIA

Company C
Henry Daton—WIA
Charles Hanna—WIA
Asahel Horton—WIA
David Lockwood—KIA
Thomas Mooney—WIA
John Osgood—WIA
Ammi Perkins—WIA
Corporal George H. Sanger—WIA
John A. Strayline—WIA

Company D
George Baker—WIA
Corporal Henry Blakeslee—WIA
William Blakeslee—WIA
Alonzo Camp—WIA
Harvey Carpenter—WIA
William Cluckey—WIA
1st Sergeant William Dudley—KIA
Corporal George Knapp—WIA
John Leffingwill—WIA
Harvey E. Pond—WIA
Corporal John Putney—WIA
Hosea Webster—WIA

Company E
Peter Ascher—WIA

Company E (cont'd.)
Charles Carroll—WIA
Christopher Fisher—WIA
Corporal Gurdin Franklin—KIA
Charles Gath—KIA
Henry Matthews—WIA
Henry J. Schrauder—WIA
Charles Welton—KIA

Company F
Augustus Palmer—KIA

Company G
1st Sergeant John Millin—WIA

Company H
Lorenzo Curtis—WIA
Peter De Caspasy—WIA
Francis Head—WIA
Patrick King—WIA
Patrick Sullivan—WIA
Corporal Jackson L. Wallace—WIA

Company I
Jerome Cheesbro—WIA
Philo Clayton—WIA
David Close—KIA
Sergeant William Lawn—WIA
Peter Nittler—WIA
Corporal Russel Wescott—WIA

Company K
Hugh Bradon—WIA
1st Sergeant William Church—KIA
Peter Connor—WIA
Alexander Mathews—WIA
Patrick Russell—WIA
Evert Voorhies—KIA

Appendix D

Losses for September 1864
Company A
William Boulton—DES—29th

Company B
Peter Cady—DES—24th
Edwin Luce—DSGD Wound—29th

Company C
Daniel Mardle—DES—27th

Company D
Nelson Frederick—DOD—13th
Charles Hickey—DSGD—26th
George Robinson—DES—27th
Corporal Daniel Wood—DSGD
    DIS—1st

Company E
John Walter—DES—22nd
Thomas Williams—DES—27th

Company F
Francis Hogan—DES—22nd
Jacob Stieh—DOW—8th
John Williams—DES—27th

Company I
William Elwood—DIED—25th
Joseph Ryan—DES—22nd
Charles Bennett—DES—22nd

Company K
John Bark—DES—22nd

Losses for October 1864
Company A
Hiram Hitchcock—VRC—7th

Company C
Leverett Hitchcock—VRC—7th

Company E
Thomas O,Maley—DSGD
    DIS—18th
Elonzo H. Jenks—ABS SICK—31st
Sergeant Charles Stevens—DSGD
    DIS—18th

Company F
Cornelius Donovan—VRC—7th
Peter Drake—VRC—7th

Company H
John McDonald—DSGD DIS—5th

Company I
David B. Price—DOW—
    hospital—18th

Company K
Nelson Doyle—ABS SICK—31st
Isaac N. Strong—DSGD—29th

Staff
Surgeon Hovey Bleecker—
    MO—19th

Appendix E

Monthly Returns
November 1862—December 1864
and
May 1865

November 1862
Present: 664   Detached: 6 officers/33 men
AWOL: 41 men   Sick: 8 officers/185 men
Total on rolls: 937

December 1862
Present: 660   Detached: 2 officers/25 men   On Leave: 7 men
AWOL: 1 officer/38 men   Sick: 4 officers/183 men
Under Arrest: 1 man   Total on rolls: 921

January 1863
Present: 629   Detached: 1 officer/29 men   On Leave: 1 officer/1 man
AWOL: 43 men   Sick: 2 officers/171 men
Under Arrest: 2 men   Total on rolls: 879

February 1863
Present: 638   Detached: 34 men   On Leave: 4 officers/1 man
AWOL: 39 men   Sick: 2 officers/129 men
Under Arrest: 1 man   Total on rolls: 848

March 1863
Present: 600   Detached: 34 men   On Leave: 6 officers/12 men
AWOL: 21 men   Sick: 99 men
Under Arrest: 2 men   Total on rolls: 774

April 1863
Present: 603   Detached: 51 men
AWOL: 18 men   Sick: 75 men
Total on rolls: 747

May 1863
Present: 599   Detached: 1 officer/38 men   On Leave: 5 officers/9 men
AWOL: 10 men   Sick: 75 men
Total on rolls: 735

June 1863
Present: 556 Detached: 3 officers/43 men On Leave: 1 officer
AWOL: 9 men Sick: 2 officers/107 men
Under Arrest: 2 men Total on rolls: 723

July 1863
Present: 423 Detached: 5 officers/54 men
AWOL: 6 men Sick: 2 officers/151 men
Total on rolls: 641

August 1863
Present: 425 Detached: 4 officers/61 men On Leave: 1 officer
AWOL: 7 men Sick: 137 men
Total on rolls: 635

September 1863
Present: 415 Detached: 4 officers/72 men
AWOL: 4 men Sick: 126 men
Total on rolls: 621

October 1863
Present: 414 Detached: 4 officers/75 men
AWOL: 4 men Sick: 121 men
Paroled: 1 man Total on rolls: 616

November 1863
Present: 395 Detached: 4 officers/72 men On Leave: 1 officer
AWOL: 1 officer/4 men Sick: 5 officers/143 men
Under Arrest: 1 man Total on rolls: 626

December 1863
Present: 421 Detached 4 officers/75 men
AWOL: 5 men Sick: 2 officers/112 men
Under Arrest: 1 man Total on rolls: 620

January 1864
Present: 542 Detached: 7 officers/126 men On Leave: 4 officers/2 men
AWOL: 4 men Sick: 1 officer/112 men
Under Arrest: 1 man Total on rolls: 799

February 1864
Present: 498 Detached: 8 officers/131 men On Leave: 2 officers/5 men
AWOL: 1 officer/1 man Sick:1 officer/114 men
Under Arrest: 2 men Total on rolls: 763

APPENDIX E

March 1864
Present: 383   Detached: 7 officers/70 men   On Leave: 1 officer/72 men
AWOL: 1 officer/1 man   Sick: 2 officers/84 men
Under Arrest: 2 men   Total on rolls: 623

April 1864
Present: 423   Detached: 8 officers/78 men   On Leave: 7 men
AWOL: 1 officer/1 man   Sick: 1 officer/69 men
Under Arrest: 2 men   Total on rolls: 590

May 1864
Present: 300   Detached: 7 officers/82 men   On Leave: 5 men
AWOL: 1 officer/2 men   Sick: 3 officers/165 men
Under Arrest: 1 man   Total on rolls: 566

June 1864
Present: 284   Detached: 7 officers/83 men   On Leave: 1 officer/4 men
AWOL: 1 officer/1 man   Sick: 2 officers/166 men
Under Arrest: 1 man   Total on rolls: 550

July 1864
Present: 286 men   Detached: 7 officers/78 men   On Leave: 4 men
AWOL: 1 officer/1 man   Sick: 3 officers/177 men
Total on rolls: 557

August 1864
Present: 250   Detached: 6 officers/80 men   On Leave: 1 officer/6 men
Sick: 3 officers/188 men   Under Arrest: 1 man
Captured: 2 men   Total on rolls: 537

September 1864
Present: 277   Detached: 6 officers/77 men   On Leave: 2 officers/7 men
Sick: 2 officers/156 men
Under Arrest: 2 men   Total on rolls: 529

October 1864
Present: 277   Detached: 5 officers/75 men   On Leave: 5 men
Sick: 2 officers/162 men
Under Arrest: 2 men   Total on rolls: 528

November 1864
Present: 271   Detached: 5 officers/76 men   On Leave: 5 men
Sick: 2 officers/171 men
Under Arrest: 1 man   Total on rolls: 531

December 1864
Present: 275   Detached: 6 officers/83 men   On Leave: 1 man
AWOL: 5 men   Sick: 2 officers/178 men
Under Arrest: 1 man   Total on rolls: 551

May 1865
Present: 286   Detached: 5 officers/81 men   On Leave: 1 officer/10 men
AWOL: 2 men   Sick: 172 men
Under Arrest: 2 men   Total on rolls: 559

Appendix F

Losses According to the Regimental Roster

September 1862
DIED: 1   DES: 9   DSGD DIS: 1   DSGD: 2   TOTAL: 13

October 1862
DIED: 1   DES: 5   DSGD DIS: 2   TOTAL: 8

November 1862
DIED: 4   DOD: 3   DES: 2   DSGD DIS: 8   DSGD:1   TOTAL: 18

December 1862
DIED: 2   DOD: 10   DES: 4   DSGD DIS: 18   DSGD: 4   TOTAL: 38

TOTAL 1862
DIED: 8   DOD: 13   DES: 20   DSGD DIS: 29   DSGD: 7   TOTAL: 77

January 1863
DIED: 2   DOD: 3   DES: 4   DSGD DIS: 14   DSGD: 15   VRC: 2   MIA/CIA: 1   TOTAL: 41

February 1863
DIED: 4   DOD: 2   DSGD DIS: 21   DSGD: 7   TOTAL: 34

March 1863
DIED: 1   DOD: 7   DES: 2   DSGD DIS: 27   DSGD: 5   TOTAL: 42

April 1863
DES: 2   DSGD DIS: 10   DSGD: 2   VRC: 1   ABS: 2   TOTAL: 17

May 1863
DES: 3   DSGD DIS: 4   DSGD: 3   ABS: 1   MIA/CIA: 1   KIA: 1   TOTAL: 13

June 1863
DES: 4   DSGD DIS: 2   DSGD: 1   ABS: 1   TOTAL: 8

July 1863
DOD: 1   DES: 15   DSGD DIS: 2   DSGD: 1   ABS: 5   MIA/CIA: 5
DOW: 6   KIA: 16   TOTAL: 51

August 1863
DES: 1   DSGD DIS: 3   DSGD: 3   VRC: 1   DOW: 3   TOTAL: 11

September 1863
DIED: 1   DES: 2   DSGD DIS: 4   VRC: 6   MIA/CIA: 1   KIA: 1
TOTAL: 15

October 1863
DES: 1   DSGD DIS: 2   DSGD: 1   VRC: 1   KIA: 2   TOTAL: 7

November 1863
DIED: 1   DSGD: 2   VRC: 5   DOW: 1   KIA: 1   TOTAL: 10

December 1863
DIED: 2   DOD: 2   DSGD DIS: 3   VRC: 1   DOW: 2   TOTAL: 10

TOTAL 1863
DIED: 11   DOD: 15   DES: 34   DSGD DIS: 92   DSGD: 40   VRC: 17
ABS: 9   MIA/CIA: 8   DOW: 12   KIA: 21   TOTAL: 259

January 1864
DOD: 2   DSGD DIS: 4   DSGD: 3   VRC: 1   TOTAL: 10

February 1864
DIED: 3   DOD: 5   DSGD DIS: 2   DSGD: 2   TOTAL: 12

March 1864
DIED: 2   DOD: 2   DSGD DIS: 2   DSGD: 3   VRC: 7   TOTAL: 16

April 1864
DOD: 4   DSGD DIS: 3   VRC: 4   TOTAL: 11

May 1864
DOD: 1   DES: 1   DSGD DIS: 1   VRC: 6   ABS: 3   MIA/CIA: 1
DOW: 5   KIA: 14   TOTAL: 32

June 1864
DOD: 2   DSGD: 2   VRC: 1   ABS: 1   MIA/CIA: 1   DOW: 4   KIA: 1
TOTAL: 12

July 1864
DOD: 2   DSGD DIS: 2   DSGD: 1   VRC: 3   ABS: 2   DOW: 3
KIA: 1   TOTAL: 14

August 1864
DIED: 1   DOD: 2   DSGD: 1   VRC: 1   ABS: 2   MIA/CIA: 2
DOW: 1   KIA: 2   TOTAL: 12

September 1864
DOD: 1   DES: 11   DSGD DIS: 2   DSGD: 1   DOW: 1   TOTAL: 16

October 1864
DSGD DIS: 3   DSGD: 1   VRC: 4   ABS: 2   DOW: 1   TOTAL: 11

November 1864
DOD: 1   DSGD DIS: 2   VRC: 3   MIA/CIA: 2   TOTAL: 8

December 1864
DES: 1   DSGD DIS: 2   VRC: 2   ABS: 1   MIA/CIA: 1   TOTAL: 7

1865
DOD: 2   DES: 4   DSGD DIS: 18   DSGD: 26   VRC: 14   ABS: 24
MIA/CIA: 6   DOW: 2   KIA: 2   TOTAL: 98

TOTAL 1864-1865
DIED: 6   DOD: 24   DES: 17   DSGD DIS: 41   DSGD: 40   VRC: 46
ABS: 35   MIA/CIA: 13   DOW: 17   KIA: 20   TOTAL: 259

TOTAL FOR 1862-1865
DIED: 25   DOD: 52   DES: 71   DSGD DIS: 162   DSGD: 87
VRC: 63   ABS: 44   MIA/CIA: 21   DOW: 29   KIA: 41   TOTAL: 595

DIED: 4%   DOD: 9%   DES: 12%   DSGD DIS: 27%   DSGD: 15%
VRC: 10%   ABS: 7%   MIA/CIA: 4%   DOW: 5%   KIA: 7%

Bibliography

A Record of the Commissioned Officers, Non-Commissioned Officers and Privates of the Regiments Which Were Organized in the State of New York, Vol. I, III, IV.

Adams, Z. Boylston, "In the Wilderness," *Civil War Papers, Read Before the Commandery of the Loyal Legion of the United States*, Vol. II, Boston, 1900.

Annual Report of the Adjutant General of the State of New York for the Year 1895, Vols. 1, 2, 3, 27, Wynkoop, Hallenbeck, Crawford & Co., State Printers, Albany, NY, 1896.

Bandy, Ken and Florence Freeland, (ed.), *The Gettysburg Papers*, Vol. III, Morningside Bookshop, Dayton, OH, 1978.

Barnhart, Clarence L., (ed in chief), *The World Book Encyclopedia Dictionary*, Vol. 1, Field Enterprises Educational Corporation, Chicago, 1964.

Bridgwater, William and Elizabeth J. Sherwood, (ed.), *The Columbia Encyclopedia in One Volume*, Columbia University Press, NY, 1950.

Census of Population, Lima, Livingston County, NY (National Archives Microfilm, roll 778) Records of the Census, Western New York.

Cooke, S. A., et al., *The Cambridge Ancient History*, Vol. XII, University Press, Cambridge, 1965.

Doty, Lockwood R., (ed.), *History of Livingston County*, W. J. Van Deusen, Publisher, Jackson, MI.

Johnson, Allen, and Dumas Malone, (ed.), *Dictionary of American Biography*, Vol. I, III, VII, Charles Scribner's Sons, NY.

Johnson, Robert Underwood and Clarence C. Buel, (ed.), *Battles and Leaders of the Civil War*, Castle, Secaucus, NJ, 4 volumes.

Office of the Adjutant General, Record Group 94, Volunteer Organizations of the Civil War, New York 136th Inf., Field and Staff, "Descriptive Rolls," National Archives, Washington, DC.

Office of the Adjutant General, Record Group 94, Muster Rolls, Returns, Regimental Papers, Volunteer Organizations of the Civil War, Boxes, 3294 and 3295, New York, 136th Inf., Return for October 1862 through April 1865, National Archives, Washington, DC.

Office of the Adjutant General, Record Group 94, Volunteer Organizations of the Civil War, New York, 136th Inf., Regimental Order and Guard Report Book, National Archives, Washington, DC.

The Adjutant General, *Massachusetts Soldiers, Sailors, and Marines in the Civil War*, Vol. III, Norwood Press, Norwood, MA, 1932.

The Official Records of the War of the Rebellion, Vol. XXXI, Part 1; XXXVIII, Part 2.

Phisterer, Frederick, (comp.), *New York in the War of the Rebellion 1861—1865*, 3rd Ed., Vols. I, II, III, IV, J. B. Lyon Co., State Printers, Albany, NY, 1912.

Regimental History of the First New York Dragoons, Gibson Brothers, Printers, Washington, DC, 1865.

Smith, James H., *1687 History of Livingston County New York*, D. Mason & Co., Syracuse, NY, 1881.

Stephen, Sir Leslie, and Sir Sidney Lee, (ed.), *Dictionary of National Biography*, Vol. XX, Oxford University Press, London, 1964.

Warner, Ezra J., *Generals in Blue*, Louisiana State University Press, Baton Rouge, LA, 1959.

Warner, Ezra J., *Generals in Gray*, Louisiana State University Press, Baton Rouge, LA, 1959.

INDEX

A

Ackerman, Ira (Pvt., Co. D) — 77
Adams, John Quincy (Pvt., Co. F) — 79
Adams, Nathan (Pvt., Co. H) — 41
Agard, Fernando W. (Pvt., Co. M, 130th NY) — 24, 37
Albro, Ruel (Pvt., Co. A) — 120
Albro, William (Pvt., Co. D) — 76
Aldie, VA — 57
Alexandria, VA — 64
Alger, Duane (Pvt., Co. I) — 41
Allen, Christopher (Pvt., Co. A) — 76
Altoft, William (Pvt., Co. D) — 115
Anderson, Martin (Pvt., Co. B) — 119
Anderson, TN — 66
Annis, Monroe (Cpl., Co. C) — 85
Arlington Heights, VA — 27
Aten, Isaac (Pvt., Co. C) — 41
Athens, GA — 72, 73
Atlanta, GA (Campaign for:) — v, 88, 110
Atwood, Carlos (Pvt., Co. G) — 41
Atwood, Garry (Pvt., Co. H) — 41
Augusta, GA — 110
Austin, Clark (Pvt., Co. H) — 83
Ayling, William (Pvt., Co. E) — 117

B

Babcock, W. Seymore (Pvt., Co. B) — 118
Bacon, James (Pvt., Co. B) — 118
Baker, Edward D. (Col., U.S. Vols.) — 4, 9
Baker, George (Pvt., Co. D) — 120
Baker, Jephthah (Pvt., Co. D) — 39
Baker, John J. (Pvt., Co. H) — 76
Baker, John P. (Pvt., Co. K) — 118
Ball's Bluff, VA — 4, 9
Baltimore, MD — 65
Bangs, P. (Reverend) — 18
Bank's Ford, VA — 42
Barber, Harrison (1st Sgt., Co. K) — 79
Barber, Zack (Pvt., Co. K) — 82
Barnard, Charles (Pvt. Co. G) — 75
Barnes, Zedrick (Pvt., Co. D) — 76
Barnhart, James (Pvt., Co. C) — 39
Barnhart, Joseph (Pvt., Co. I) — 78
Bartlett, Myron (1st Lt., Co. D) — 38
Bass, George (1st Lt., Co. K) — 77
Bassett, Charles (Pvt., Co. E) — 75
Beach, Wooster (Doctor) — 15, 35
Beckly, _____ (Co. D, 126th NY) — 50
Beedle, Charles (Sgt., Co. I) — 115

Berlin, MD — 56, 64
Bertram, Philip (Pvt., Co. I) — 75
Billings, Delos (Cpl., Co. K) — 83
Bishop, Herbert (Pvt., Co. G) — 75
Bliss, Edwin (Cpl., Co. A) — 115
Bough, John (Governor, OH) — 64
Bow, Myron (Pvt., Co. G) — 77
Bowen, John (Pvt., Co. D) — 117
Bowen, Samuel (Pvt., Co. H) — 76
Bowling Green, KY — 64
Boyd, John, Jr. (Sgt., Co. H) — 86
Bracey, Elisha (Pvt., Co. D) — 80
Bradley, Lucius (Cpl., Co. B) — 83
Bradon, James (Pvt., Co. K) — 120
Bragdon, E. E. E. (Reverend — 12, 17, 18, 34
Bragg, Braxton (Gen., C.S.A.) — 67, 70, 85
Branseau (Gen., U.S.A.) — 104
Bratton (Confederate Governor of Georgia) — 111
Brenan, Martin (Pvt., Co. C) — 76
Bridgeport, OH — 64
Bridgeport, TN — 67, 68
Briggs, James (Pvt., Co. C) — 85
Brintsville, VA — 59
Bristoe Station, VA — 49, 61, 64
Bristol, George (Pvt., Co. C) — 85
Bristol, John (Pvt., Co. B) — 86
Britton, Homer (Pvt., Co. C) — 39
Britton, Johnathan (Pvt., Co C) — 85
Brough, John — 83
Broughton, Harrison (Cpl., Co. H) — 75
Brown, Andrew (Pvt., Co. A) — 83
Brown, Murray (Pvt., Co. C) — 41
Brownell, Horace (Pvt., Co. D) — 75
Buck Head, GA — 118
Buckley, Dennis (Pvt., Co. G) — 104, 119
Buckner, Simon B. (Gen., C.S.A.) — 17, 35
Buell, Seth P. (2nd Lt., Cpt., Co. E) — 24, 26, 37, 80
Bull Run, (Manassas), VA — 29, 30, 62, 63
Bullard, Robert F. (2nd Lt., Co. I) — 85, 118
Bulson, Stephen (Pvt., Co. K) — 83
Burke, Robert (Pvt., Co. H) — 77
Burns, John (Pvt., Co. C) — 119
Burnside, Ambrose (Gen., U.S.A.) — 33, 42, 72
Burr, Elliott (Pvt., Co. K) — 40
Bush, _____, Miss (civilian, Lima, NY) — 60

INDEX 137

Butterfield, Daniel (Gen., U.S.A.) — 93
Buzzard's Roost, GA — 93

C

Callaghan, Neil (Cpl., Co. D) — 76
Cameron, James (Cpt., Co. D) — 115
Camp, Griffin (Pvt., Co. D) — 76
Card, Coryden (Pvt., Co., D) — 75
Carpenter, Charles (Pvt., Co. E) — 75
Carroll, Charles (Pvt., Co. E) — 117
Carroll,Thomas (Pvt., Co. H) — 41
Case (Professor) — 7
Casey, Anthony (Pvt., Co. F) — 39
Casualties at Resaca, GA, May 15, 1864 — 125
Catlett Station, VA — 58, 59, 61
Centreville, OH — 64
Centreville, VA — 29, 50
Chamberlin, Henry (Pvt., Co. D) — 78
Chancellorsville, VA — v, 47-48
Chapin, Willard (Cpt., Co. C) — 116
Chapman, John (Pvt., Co. E) — 41
Chapman, Peter (Pvt., Co. F) — 118
Chappell, George Henry (Pvt., Co. G, 27th NY) — 56, 81
Charleston, TN — 72, 73
Chase, Kate — 30
Chase, Salmon P. (Sec. of the Treasury) — 30
Chattahoochie River, GA — 103, 107, 118
Chattanooga, TN — 67, 69, 70, 73, 74, 91, 92, 111
Chickamauga Creek, GA — 73
Churchill, Homer (Cpl., Co. A) — 39
Clark, Robert (Pvt., Co. B) — 83
Clemens, Harrison (Pvt., Co. I) — 117
Cleveland, Henry (Pvt., Co. H) — 39
Cleveland, TN — 71, 73
Clinton, Thomas (Pvt., Co. D) — 75
Close, William (Pvt., Co. I) — 118
Clow, Benjamin (Pvt., Co. E) — 78
Clute, Andrew (Pvt., Co. F) — 117
Coffee, Charles (Pvt., Co. E) — 79
Cole, Alvin (Cpt., Co. A) — 41, 97
Cole, George (Musician, Co. B) — 80
Cole, Thomas (Musician, Co. B) — 76
Coleman, V. Bemis (Sgt., Co. A) — 84
College Hall, Lima, NY — 2, 7, 16
Columbus, OH — 64, 65
Compton, James (Pvt., Co. I) — 83
Conger, Nathaniel (Pvt., Co. H) — 86
Connor, Nicholas (Pvt., Co. E) — 86
Coon, George (Pvt., Co. K) — 118
Corbin, Daniel (Pvt., Co. K) — 76
Cornell, Alanson B. (Cpt., Co. G, 130th NY) — 24, 37
Cowley, Covel (Pvt., Co. E) — 81

Cross Theron (1st Sgt., Co. K) — 119
Crowel, Edward (Pvt., Co. D) — 119
Culvor, James (Pvt., Co. B) — 78
Culvor, James (Pvt., Co. D) — 40
Cumberland, MD — 64, 65
Cummings, John (Pvt., Co. D) — 77
Curtis, Henry (Pvt., Co. E) — 118
Curtis, John (Pvt., Co. D) — 77
Curtis, Lorenzo (Pvt., Co. H) — 120

D

Dallas-Marietta Road, GA — 117
Danforth, Patrick (Pvt., Co. H) — 39
Dart, William, Pvt., Co. F — 76
Davidsberg, GA — 112
Davie, Louis (Pvt., Co. A) — 41
Davis, Amos (Cpt., Co. K) — 39
Davis, Whipple (Cpl., Co. I) — 116
Dayton, Lewis (Pvt., Co. C) — 40
Dayton, OH — 64, 65
Dean, Oliver (Pvt., Co. I) — 115
Decker, James (Pvt., Co. C) — 118
Decker, M. (enlistee) — 26
Denison, Henry (Pvt., Co. C) — 75
Dewey, Oliver (Pvt., Co. D) — 76
Dieffenbacher, Florus (Pvt., Co. G) — 75
Dieter, Jacob (Sgt., Co. I) — 116
Dippy, George (Cpl., Co. B) — 78
Dodge, Devillo A. (Pvt., Co. E) — 91
Doerflinger, William (Pvt., Co. I) — 84
Dogwood Valley, GA — 92
Doren, James (Pvt., Co. E) — 53
Dorr, Faulkner (Cpl., Co. B) — 83
Doty, Zebulon (Pvt., Co. G) — 77
Dow, James (Pvt., Co. E) — 118
Dow, Robert (Cpl., Co. E) — 75
Drehmer, George (Pvt., Co. B) — 119
Dudley, Harlow (Pvt., Co. H) — 115
Dudley, Russell (1st Lt., Co. D) — 75
Duffy, Patrick (Pvt., Co. E) — 53
Dumfries, VA — 33
Dunbar, Jonas (Pvt., Co. H) — 76
Dunn, James (Pvt., Co. G) — 76

E

Eager, Avery (Pvt., Co. D) — 115
Eastman, Alvarado (Pvt., Co. A) — 40
Easton, Thomas (Pvt., Co. B) — 80
Ecclesiastical History, 12
Eddy, Alonzo (Pvt., Co. C) — 41
Edwards' Ferry, VA — 51
Eker, Mathias (Pvt., Co. H) — 117
Ellison, William (Pvt., Co. F) — 120
Elmer, Nathan (Pvt., Co. C) — 40
Elwell, James (Pvt., Co. H) — 79
Emery, Homer (Sgt., Co. D) — 116
Emmitsburg, MD — 53, 54
Eusebius — v, 12, 34

F

Fairfax Court House, VA — 4, 29, 31, 32
Family Physician — 15
Fanning, James (Cpl., Co. G) — 119
Farmington, MD — 64
Ferris, Dwight (Pvt., Co. A) — 83, 120
Fiero, John (Cpl., Co. E) — 53
Finch, Joseph (Pvt., Co. A) — 83
Finn, Patrick (Pvt., Co. B) — 119
Fish, Reuben (Pvt., Co. A) — 75
Fisk, Wilbur (Reverend) — 18, 36
Flint, Frank (Pvt., Co. D) — 78
Flint, William (Pvt., Co. D) — 119
Floyd, James B. (Gen., C.S.A.) — 17, 35
Folmsbee, John (Pvt., Co. G) — 82
Foote, Baldess (Pvt., Co. B) — 80
Foote, Seeley (Pvt., Co. H) — 118
Fort Donelson, TN — 17, 34, 35
Fort Henry, TN — 15, 34
Foster, Daniel (Chaplain, 33rd MA) — 82
Franklin, KY — 65
Frederick City, MD — 51
Fredericksburg, VA — 33, 47
Fremont, John C. (Gen., U.S. Vols.) — 4, 9-10
French, James (Pvt., Co. F) — 76
Fricker (Reverend) — 2
Funkstown, MD — 55
Futeki, *Physical Geography* — 14

G

Gage, Joshua (Pvt., Co. B) — 82
Gainsville, VA — 30
Galbraith, John (Cpl., Co. F) — 75
Galbraith, John J. (1st Lt., Co., F) — 39, 41
Gale, Henry (2nd Lt., Co. B, 130th NY) — 56, 62, 81-82
Galentine, Jacob S. (QM) — 72, 86
Gannon, Anthony (Pvt., Co. G) — 40
Gardner, Alexander (Pvt., Co. A) — 76
Gardner, Dennis (Pvt., Co. A) — 76
Gardner, Hermann (Pvt., Co. A) — 84
Garthwait, Daniel (Pvt., Co. K) — 41
Gatz, Jacob (Pvt., Co. H) — 76
Gavagan, John (Pvt., Co. B) — 116
Gay, Manilus (Pvt., Co. E) — 80
Geary, John W. (Gen., U.S.A.) — 70
Genesee Wesleyan Seminary, Lima, NY — 7, 11, 17, 18, 26
German, Derious (Pvt., Co. K) — 115
Gernsey, Levi (Pvt., Co. H) — 120
Gettysburg, PA — v, 53-54, 79-80, 101, 122-123
Gibbs, Harvey (Pvt., Co. C) — 75
Gibbs, Norman (Pvt., Co. I) — 77

Gill, John (Pvt., Co. I) — 115
Glease, C. (Reverend) — 4
Goodwin, William H. (Reverend) — 1, 8
Goose Creek, VA — 50, 57
Gordon's Mills, GA — 92
Gottschall, George (Pvt., Co. B) — 118
Gould, Chester (Pvt., Co. C) — 75
Graham, James (Pvt., Co. F) — 76
Graham, Martin (Pvt., Co. D) — 118
Grant, Ulysses S. (Gen., U.S.A.) — 67, 71
Grant, William (Pvt., Co. H) — 115
Gray, Reuben (Pvt., Co. E) — 77
Green, Robert (Pvt., Co. F) — 119
Greenwich, VA — 61
Grely, Michael (Pvt., Co. F) — 76
Griffith, Wallace (Pvt., Co. D) — 118
Grills, William (Pvt., Co. C) — 41
Gurgen, Nicholas (Pvt., Co. B) — 84

H

Hagerstown, MD — 55, 56
Hall, Anson (1st Lt., Co. H) — 115
Hall, Elijah (Pvt., Co. A) — 77
Hall, James (Pvt., Co. G) — 87
Hall, William (1st Lt., Co. A) — 116, 117
Hall, _____, Mr. (civilian, Lima, NY) — 60
Hamilton, Norman (Pvt., Co. C) — 75
Hammond, John (Pvt., Co. C) — 115
Hanigan, James (Sgt., Co. E) — 53, 60
Hann, Louis (Pvt., Co. B) — 41
Harding, Charles (Pvt., Co. B, 130th NY) — 56, 62, 81
Harmon, Charles (Pvt., Co. A) — 39
Harper's Ferry, WV — 56, 64
Harrington, Augustus (Cpt., Co. D) — 75
Harrington, Charles H. (2nd Lt., Co. D) — 77
Harris, William (Pvt., Co. B) — 83
Hartshorn, Davis C. (Maj.) — 27, 79
Hartwood Church, VA — 49
Haskins, John (Pvt., Co. A) — 76
Hatch, Washington (Cpl., Co. A) — 77
Havens, Henry (Pvt., Co. I) — 78
Hay Market, VA — 30, 31
Hayen, John (Cpl., Co. G) — 83
Heller, John (Pvt., Co. B) — 116
Heminway, DeWitt (Pvt., Co. E) — 77
Hendershott, Wells (Cpt., Co. D) — 79
Hendrick, John (Pvt., Co. F) — 117
Hendrickson, William (Pvt., Co. K) — 120
Henry, James (Pvt., Co. C) — 81
Henry, Jerome (Pvt., Co. I) — 75
Herdendorf, Elisha (Pvt., Co. E) — 117, 119
Hewitt, William (Pvt., Co. F) — 80

INDEX

Higgins, Ezra (Pvt., Co. D) — 40
Hill, William (Pvt., Co. G) — 79
Hitchcock, Hiram (Pvt., Co. A) — 119
Hiwassee River, GA — 72
Hoffman, Delos (Pvt., Co. A) — 77
Hollowell, George (Pvt., Co. C) — 41
Holmes, William (Pvt., Co. A) — 76
Honeoye Falls, NY — 24
Hooker, Joseph (MG, U.S.A.) — 44, 46, 48, 67, 70, 74, 76, 93
Horton, Charles (QM) — 40
Hotchkiss, Aaron (Pvt., Co. K) — 77
House, Charles (Pvt., Co. B, 130th NY) — 56, 62, 82
Howard, Oliver O. (Gen., U.S.A.) — 46, 67, 70, 78, 85
Howell, Addison (Pvt., Co. K) — 78
Hoxie, Watson (Pvt., Co. D) — 39
Hoyt, Almon (Cpt., Co. C) — 79
Hoyt, Elias (Cpl., Co. D) — 115
Hoyt, Emerson (1st Lt., Co. C) — 79
Huggins, William (Cpl., Co. F) — 84
Hull, Daniel V. (Pvt., Co. G) — 81
Hurd, Lewis (Professor) — 2, 8

I

Ikins, Simeon (Pvt., Co. K) — 83
Indianapolis, IN — 64, 65
Ives (Reverend) — 17

J

Jackson, Robert (Pvt., Co. C) — 82
Jefferson, MD — 51, 56
Jeffersonville, IN — 65
Jeffres, Ezra (Cpt., Co. H) — 75
Jenks, Henry B. (Cpt., Co. E) — 26, 38, 77
Jetty, William (Pvt., Co. A) — 119
Jincks, Daniel (Sgt., Co. D) — 84
Johnson, Bushrod R. (Gen., C.S.A.) — 17, 35
Johnson, Daniel (Pvt., Co. G) — 77
Johnson, Frank (Cpl., Co. E) — 77
Johnson, Isaac (1st Lt., Co. D) — 115
Johnson, Joel (Pvt., Co. I) — 77
Johnson, John (Pvt., Co. D) — 82
Jones, Charles (Pvt., Co. K) — 80
Jones, Henry (Pvt., Co. G) — 115
Jones, James (Pvt., Co. G) — 117
Joslyn, Marshal (Pvt., Co. H) — 79
Joslyn Willard (Pvt., Co. H) — 79

K

Keel, Edward (Pvt., Co. D) — 115
Keiper, Gaskard (Pvt., Co. G) — 119
Kellogg, Edward (Cpl., Co. D) — 116
Kellogg, John (Pvt., Co. K) — 79
Kelly, James (Pvt., Co. F) — 117

Kelly, John (Pvt., Co. F) — 79
Kelly's Ford, VA — 47
Kiehle, James (Pvt., Co. I) — 40
Kneeland, Benjamin T. (Surg., 130th NY) — 24, 37
Kneip, Dominique (Pvt., Co. G) — 117
Knowles, Daniel C. (Cpt., Co. D, 48th NY) — 5, 11
Knowles, Joseph H. (Reverend) — 2, 3, 5, 6, 8, 17
Knowlton, Marcus (Pvt., Co. K) — 119
Knoxville, TN — 72, 74
Kuhn, George (Pvt., Co. I) — 117

L

Lafosce, Jacob (Pvt., Co. B) — 118
Landen, Jacob (Pvt., Co. G) — 77
Lane, Reuben (Pvt., Co. E) — 78
Lavery, James (Pvt., Co. E) — 53, 80, 117
Lawton, Robers (Pvt., Co. H) — 85
Layden, Marshall M. (1st Lt., Co. A) — 41
Lee, Robert E. (Gen., C.S.A.) — 70, 85
Leesburg, VA — 50, 56
Lester, John (Pvt., Co. E) — 75
Levers, Thomas (Pvt., Co. B) — 82
Lewis, Gilbert (Pvt., Co. I) — 76
Lewis, John (Pvt., Co. B) — 117, 118
Lexington, MO — 1, 8
Lima, NY — 24, 80
Limerick, Henry (Pvt., Co. F) — 80
Lincoln, Abraham (President, U.S.A.) — 1, 46, 66
Lincoln, Thomas "Tadpole" — 78
Lincoln, William (Pvt., Co. D) — 77
Lindsley, Irving (Pvt., Co. C) — 78
Little Rock, MD — 54
Litz, Frederick (Pvt., Co. E) — 117
Locke, Orrin (Musician, Co. C) — 76
Lockwood, Isaac (Pvt., Co. B) — 81
Logan, _____ (Gen., U.S.A.) — 93
London, OH — 64, 65
Longstreet, James (Gen., C.S.A.) — 70, 71, 85
Lookout Mountain, TN — v, 67, 69, 70
Losses at Gettysburg, PA, July 2-3, 1863 — 122-123
Losses for September 1864 — 126
Losses March 1-22, 1864 — 124
Lottridge, John (2nd Lt., Co. K) — 82
Louisville, KY — 64, 65
Lousiville, TN — 72
Luce, Worthington (Pvt., Co. B) — 75
Lynch, Edward (Pvt., Co. E) — 117, 118
Lynn, Clarence (Pvt., Co. G) — 120
Lyon, Harrison (Pvt., Co. C) — 82

M

Madison, GA — 111
Madden, Edward (1st Lt., Co. H) — 75
Mann, Russell (Pvt., Co. H) — 116
Marsh, Alfred (Pvt., Co. H) — 120
Mathews, Alexander C. (Pvt., Co. K) — 117
Martinsburg, WV — 64
Maxon, Charles (Pvt., Co. H) — 120
May, James (Pvt., Co. I) — 76
Mayhew, Morgan (Pvt., Co. H) — 82
McBallard, James (Pvt., Co. A) — 77
McCarthy, Daniel (Pvt., Co. K) — 78
Macauley, Joseph (Pvt., Co. E) — 78
McClellan, George B. (Gen., U.S.A.) — 5, 10
McCoy, John (Pvt., Co. C) — 81
McCray, Harlow (Pvt., Co. H) — 79
McCray, John (Cpl., Co. H) — 115
McCullough, Henry (Pvt., Co. F) — 75
McDonald, George (Pvt., Co. I) — 40
McDowell, Irwin (Gen., U.S.A.) — 48
McFarlin, Lafayette (Pvt., Co. I) — 41
McGary, Charles (Pvt., Co. C) — 38
McGuire, Edward (Pvt., Co. E) — 82
McGuire, John (Pvt., Co. E) — 83
McGuire, Patrick (Pvt., Co. G) — 76
McKee, James (Pvt., Co. K) — 118
McKee, Joseph W. (Pvt., Co. K) — 76
McMahon, Isabell — 21, 36, 40
McMahon, Isaiah — 2, 8, 14, 27, 121
McMahon, John T. (Pvt., Co. E) — v, vi, 9, 37, 60, 114, 121
McMahon, Laura — 12, 34, 121
McMahon, Margaret M. — 5, 11
McMahon, Richard (Pvt., Co. E) — 31, 32, 36, 40
McMahon, Sarah Jane — 18, 36
McMahon, William H. (Pvt., Co. G, 27th NY) — 1, 8, 21, 36
McMartin, John (Pvt., Co. G) — 41
McPherson, James A. (Gen., U.S.A.) — 93, 96, 104
Mead, James (Pvt., Co. A) — 119
Metcalf, Chapin J. (Pvt., Co. D) — 84
Metcalf, Pliny (Cpl., Co. D) — 115
Methodist Episcopal Church (Lima, NY) — 1, 2
Middletown, MD — 51, 56
Milledgeville, GA — 111
Millhollen, William (Pvt., Co. K) — 76
Milner, Edward (Pvt., Co. H) — 118
Missionary Ridge, TN — 71, 86
Mobile, AL — 70
Moore, George (Pvt., Co. C) — 78, 84
Moore, James Harrison (Pvt., Co. D) — 83
Mosher, Albert (Pvt., Co. H) — 39
Mosher, George (Pvt., Co. H) — 82
Mundy, Nicholas (2nd Lt., Co. B) — 75
Munger, Jerome (Cpl., Co. K) — 41
Munsee, William (Pvt., Co. I) — 40
Murray, Houghton (Sgt., Co. G) — 40
Murray, John (Pvt., Co. E) — 41
Mus, Peter (Pvt., Co. H) — 116

N

Nashville, TN — 65
Natural Theology — 21, 22
Naughton, Andrew (Pvt., Co. D) — 120
Neff, Henry (Pvt., Co. G) — 115
Neff, Newton (Pvt., Co. G) — 117
Nelson, Thomas (Pvt., Co. D) — 80
New Bottom, VA — 58
New York *Tribune* — 1
Nickajack Creek, GA — 118
Nick-a-Jack Gap, GA — 92
Noyes' Greek, GA — 117

O

Oconee River, GA — 112
Ogeechee River, GA — 112
Olney, Covil (Sgt., Co. D) — 75
Oostanaula River, GA — 95
Orcutt, Andrew (Pvt., Co. E) — 76
Orr, Henry (Pvt., Co. H) — 86

P

Page, David Perkins — v, 3, 9
Palmer, _____ (Gen., U.S.A.) — 93
Papson, George (Pvt., Co. H) — 39
Parker, William (Pvt., Co. F) — 76
Pasco, Edwin (Pvt., Co. K) — 76
Paul, James B. (Pvt., Co. H) — 116
Peach Tree Creek, GA — v, 104, 118-119
Pearson, Seward (Pvt., Co. B) — 119
Pease, Charles N. (Pvt., Co. B) — 40
Peck, Warren F. (Pvt., Co. E) — 38
Peckham, Ira D. (Pvt., Co. D) — 82
Perkins, Ammi (Pvt., Co. C) — 117
Phelan, Timothy (Pvt., Co. F) — 82
Philadelphia, TN — 72, 73
Phillips, James (Musician, Co. E) — 77
Pillow, Gideon J. (Gen., C.S.A.) — 17, 35
Plants, John V. (Pvt., Co. A) — 87
Pleasant Valley, GA — 92
Polen, William (Cpl., Co. I) — 76
Pond, Benjamin (Pvt., Co. D) — 118
Pond, Harvey E. (Pvt., Co. D) — 117
Poolesville, MD — 51
Porst, William H. (Pvt., Co. I) — 86
Portage, NY — 24, 26
Post, Jacob (Pvt., Co. F) — 118
Potomac River, MD — 51, 55, 56, 101

INDEX 141

Potter, Joel M. (Pvt., Co. H) — 75
Powers, Charles (Pvt., Co. K) — 79
Pratt, Edward (Cpt., Co. B) — 119
Price, David B. (Pvt., Co. I) — 119

Q

Quick, Charles (Pvt., Co. B) — 75
Quigley, Martin (Cpl., Co. C) — 83

R

Randall, Charles R. (Pvt., Co. H) — 76
Rappahannock River, VA — 42, 47
Red Clay Station, GA — 71
Reed, Jr., Lynus (Pvt., Co. I) — 40
Regiments:
  130th New York (19th NY Cav./1st NY Drag.) — 27, 56, 62, 83; 31st Mississippi — 118; 33rd Massachusetts — 60, 65; 55th New Jersey — 72; 73rd Ohio — 118; 75th Pennsylvania — 62
Reid, John M. (Reverend) — 1, 2, 6, 8, 18
Reilly, Patrick (Pvt., Co. F) — 76
Resaca, GA — 94
Rier, _____ (Pvt., 130th NY) — 62
Roanoke Island, NC — 17
Roberts, James H. (Pvt., Co. I) — 75
Robinson, Abner (Pvt., Co. F) — 76
Rogers, John H. (Pvt., Co. B) — 76
Rogersville, GA — 95
Rolls, Joseph (Pvt., Co. A) — 75
Rosecrans, William S. (Gen., U.S.A.) — 65, 67, 83-84
Rouse, John G. (Pvt., Co. A) — 117
Rulapaugh, Gilbert (Pvt., Co. F) — 85
Russell, Alexander R. (Pvt., Co. F) — 84
Ryan, Patrick (Pvt., Co. H) — 77

S

Sackett, Jr., Orange (1st Lt., Co. G) — 39
Sandersville, GA — 112
Sandy Hill, GA — 95
Sanford, Joshua (Pvt., Co. B) — 117
Sanger, George H. (Cpl., Co. C) — 118
Sanger, John G. (Pvt., Co. C) — 40
Schrauder, Henry (Pvt., Co. E) — 117
Scott, Alanson (Pvt., Co. A) — 41
Scott, Henry F. (Pvt., Co. K) — 75
Scott, Kidder M. (Cpt., Co. H) — 79
Scott, Winfield (Gen., U.S.A.) — 5, 11
Sharow, Lewis (Pvt., Co. G) — 75
Sharples, Albert G. (Pvt., Co. F) — 78
Sherman, William T. (Gen., U.S.A.) — 93, 113
Sherwood, Ira W. (Pvt., Co. F) — 117

Shunway, Charles (Pvt., Co. F) — 38
Sickles, John W. (Pvt., Co. F) — 75
Sigel, Franz (Gen., U.S.A.) — 43, 44, 76
Sill, Edward (1st Lt., Co. K) — 117
Simons, Andrew J. (Pvt., Co. E) — 76
Sinnott, Joseph (Pvt., Co. E) — 71, 86
Skinner, Levi T. (Pvt., Co. E) — 86
Skuse, James (Pvt., Co. F) — 76
Slack, Eli (Pvt., Co. D) — 84
Slate, Eliphalet (Pvt., Co. F) — 76
Slate, James M. (Pvt., Co. F) — 115
Smith, Alturna C. (Pvt., Co. H) — 117
Smith, Charles (Pvt., Co. B) — 41
Smith, George J. (Pvt., Co. K) — 78
Smith, Joel M. W. (Musician, Co. B) — 78
Smith, John R. (Asst. Surg.) — 119
Smith, John (Pvt., Co. H) — 83
Smith, Levi G. (Pvt., Co. K) — 80
Smith, Lucien A. (1st Sgt., Co. G) — 79, 80
Smith, Lucien J. (Cpl., Co. G) — 80, 82
Smith, Norman J. (Pvt., Co. C) — 40
Smith, Orlando (Col., U.S.A., brigade of:) — 84
Snake Gap, GA — 93
Snyder, George (Pvt., Co. K) — 82, 118
Social Circle, GA — 111
Soldier's Rest, Washington, DC — 27
Sorg, William (Pvt., Co. I) — 85
Sortore, John D. (Pvt., Co. K) — 82
South Mountain Pass (Turner's Gap), MD — 51, 55
Squrbier, Jonas (Pvt., Co. I) — 76
Stack, Thomas (Pvt., Co. D) — 39
Stafford Court House, VA — 43, 48
Stannard, William W. (Pvt., Co. A) — 119
Stearns, Augustus F. (Pvt., Co. H) — 41
Stieh, Jacob (Pvt., Co. F) — 119
Stoddard, Myron W. (Pvt., Co. C) — 40
Stowell, John (Pvt., Co. H) — 80
Summers, Burr (Pvt., Co. C) — 119
Summers, Sylvester (Pvt., Co. C) — 75
Sunderlin, Daniel E. (Pvt., Co. G) — 39
Suton, George (Pvt., Co. I) — 40
Sweeten, Benjamin (Pvt., Co. E) — 79

T

Taylor, William H. H. (Pvt., Co. A) — 86
Teague, Barney (Pvt., Co. G) — 80
Teetsworth, Abram (Pvt., Co. I) — 76
Telford, George L. (Pvt., Co. D) — 117
Tennessee River, TN — 65, 67, 72
Terwilliger, M. D. (enlistee) — 26
Thomas, George H. (Gen., U.S.A.) — 70, 85, 91, 93, 115
Thomas, Morgan H. (Pvt., Co. B, 136th NY) — 39

Thoroughfare Gap, VA — 30, 31, 58
Thurstin, Daniel H. (Pvt., Co. H) — 41
Tiffany, Ephraim E. (Pvt., Co. E) — 83
Torrey, George E. (1st Sgt., Co. G, 130th NY) — 24, 56, 62, 81
Touhil, Michael (Cpl., Co. F) — 80
Tresser, Charles F. (1st Lt., Co. C) — 85, 86
True, Bishop Hamlin (2nd Lt., Co. E) — 54, 58, 68, 74, 80
True, Dan (civilian) — 90
Truesdell, William G. (Pvt., Co. A) — 78
Turner's Ferry, GA — 107

V

Van Rensselaer, Carroll (Pvt., Co. G) — 41
Van Sickle, James C. (Pvt., Co. C) — 41
Van Valkenburgh, Joseph (Co. C) — 75
Van Zandt, H. Edward (1st Lt., Co. A) — 83
Vollmer, Matthaus (Pvt., Co. D) — 80
Von Steinwehr, Adolph W. A. (Gen., U.S.A.) — 45, 77

W

Wade, David C. (Pvt., Co. I) — 115
Wakeman, Hiram G. (Pvt., Co., A) — 41
Wallace, Allen C. (Pvt., Co. C) — 77
Walldy, John (enlistee) — 24, 37
Ward, Sidney (Cpt., Co. G) — 77
Ward, William H. (Cpl., Co. C) — 118, 119
Warheight, John (Pvt., Co. H) — 117
Warner, Charles (Asst. Surgeon) — 39, 75
Warrenton Junction, VA — 58
Warriner, Charles (Cpl., Co. H) — 116
Washington, D.C. — 27, 64, 65
Waterford, VA — 57
Watertown, NY — 1
Watson, Richard (Reverend) — v, 13, 14, 34
Watson, Thomas (Pvt., Co. I) — 84
Wauhatchie, TN — 84
Weaver, Hiram (Pvt., Co. H) — 75
Webster, Hosea (Pvt., Co. H) — 120
Webster, John W. (2nd Lt., Co. A) — 75
Webster, Myron (Pvt., Co. G) — 40
Weller, David Henry (Pvt., Co. M, 8th NYHA) — 24, 37
Wells, Guilford Wiley (1st Lt., Co. G) — 56, 81
Wells, William (Professor) — 6, 11
Welstead, James (Pvt., Co. I) — 75
Wescott, George W. (Pvt., Co. I) — 83
Wescott, Russell P. (Cpl., Co. I) — 118

Weverville, VA — 49
Wheeling, WV — 64
Wheelor, James H. (Pvt., Co. K) — 75
Whipple, Daniel B. (Pvt., Co. H) — 117
White, George H. (Pvt., Co. A) — 116
White Plains, VA — 58
Whitford, George W. (Pvt., Co. E) — 41
Whitmore, Samuel (Pvt., Co. G) — 119
Wiggins, Lelotas C. (Pvt., Co. E) — 53
Williams, Barney (Pvt., Co. F) — 75
Williams, Isaac T. (Pvt., Co. G) — 116
Williams, John (Pvt., Co. F) — 115
Williams, William Z. (Pvt., Co. F) — 76
Wilson, James — 16
Wilson, Oren (Pvt., Co. D) — 120
Wilson, Samuel W. (Sgt., Co. G) — 84
Winans, Edwin (Pvt., Co. G) — 86
Wing, Henry C. (Cpl., Co. D) — 115
Wing, Horace (Pvt., Co. I) — 77
Wixon, Johnathan K. (Pvt., Co. K) — 41
Wolcott, Samuel A. (Pvt., Co. H) — 116
Wood, James, Jr. (Col.) — 27, 38, 84
Woolhiser, George (Pvt., Co. K) — 116
Worden, George T. (Pvt., Co. H) — 117
Wright, Henry H. (Pvt., Co. A) — 77
Wright, James R. (Pvt., Co. H) — 41
Wright, John T. (QM) — 41
Wright, Thomas (Pvt., Co. A) — 83
Wrin, Patrick (Pvt., Co. F) — 39

Y

Yencer, Ambrose (Pvt., Co. F) — 85
Yencer, James A. (Pvt., Co. F) — 80
Yencer, Samuel R. (Pvt., Co. F) — 117
Youells, Richard (Pvt., Co. C) — 80
Young, Campbell Harris (Adj.) — 68
Young, Samuel (Pvt., Co. I) — 76